Table of Contents

With deepest gratitude to my husband Michael, my son Marcus and my granddaughter Rachel for their unwavering support and help in getting this book launched.

Author's Note:

In the following narrative, I am telling of the terrible events that even non-Jewish families had to endure under the Hitler Regime, especially families who were not listed in the annals of the Nazis.

I am grateful for some of the photos in this book which tell their own story. I purchased them from the Archives in Solingen.

Ursula Holman

Playing in the Rubble of War
by Ursula Holman

No time to shut the door quietly. The apartment door slammed behind the grandmother and her six-year-old granddaughter. Down one flight of stairs, then the second, the long hallway and out of the main entrance door.

They ran. The goal - the bomb shelter almost a mile away.

"Ommi, why do we have to run? Are the planes coming?"

"Yes, child, hush now, we have to get to the shelter."

"I don't hear them, Ommi,"

"You will, child, please be quiet and run with Ommi as fast as you can."

They ran, panting, hearts pumping, lungs straining to provide needed oxygen.

"Ommi, I can't run anymore," with a voice too breathless to have volume.

Her grandmother dragged the child along, running, gasping for air. The child's hand slipped out of her grandmother's. She turned to find the little hand again and seeing the exhaustion of the child, scooped her up and ran. She hoped her impaired heart would last until she could bring the child to the safety of the bunker. They ran, by this time automatically, hearts racing, lungs aching, and then they heard them, the planes carrying death.

They stopped running and stepped into the first shelter they saw. The once proud department store of the Tietz family, the Kaufhof, was now just a bombed-out shell, but it provided some security. At least they could not be seen from above.

And then they heard the cacophony of destruction.

Prologue

Evil bides its time, when the time is right it morphs into a lamb seducing anyone in its path. When the intended victims have been blinded by passionate words and promises of a bright future, evil morphs into a raging beast devouring its prey.

Such evil entered Germany in 1933 in the person of an Austrian house painter whose name was Adolf Hitler. Germany's Iron Chancellor Otto von Hindenburg grudgingly ceded, and Adolf Hitler, the Austrian house painter, became Fuehrer (Leader) of the Germans practically overnight. Hitler's monstrous scheme was to present the Germans with the dream of becoming a powerful nation once again. Not too many years ago, after losing WWI in 1918, the Germans were unmercifully browbeaten by France and seemed to turn into a nation lacking pride and purpose. Hitler's promise to the German people was a one-thousand-year empire, gloriously led by himself as the savior of the nation. Hitler's lofty goal was world domination placing himself among the ranks of such notables as Napoleon Bonaparte, Alexander the Great and maybe even Caesar to name a few. History tells of these men and their initial accomplishments, then leaving thousands and even millions of victims in their destructive wake.

Hitler, although relatively uneducated, nonetheless had the magnetic personality to reach deep into the soul of almost every German. And so the Germans, after their defeat, succumbed to Hitler's and his propaganda minister Joseph Goebbels' bombastic rhetoric. Hitler became the most powerful figure in German politics at a breakneck pace. Since their utter humiliation, the Germans were praying for revenge, and Hitler promised them just that. The people were suffering from widespread unemployment and abject poverty, and the time was ripe for evil to begin its devastation.

This book is not meant to be a lesson in European history, the world has witnessed the events that led up to WWII. I wrote this book as a homage to my family, my father specifically and my hometown and to tell my story. A tale of an adventurous German girl who tried to make the best of living through turbulent times. I also hope that this

3

book would be helpful to younger readers, especially those whose parents did not return from conflict.

I was born in Solingen, a beautiful town near the Rhineland, and to me it was the best place on earth. But truth be told, and unbeknownst to me at that time, Solingen was not to be without blemish during the Hitler years. Terrible things happened even in this small, picturesque spot. However, I was a child and did not know about the evil things humanity is capable of doing. I was surrounded by a loving family and early in my life I did not have much to worry about. By the time I was five years old I had heard the adults around me speaking of war, and I did know that my father was a soldier fighting in this war. I heard people call it frightening and awful and terrible, but all that talk still did not mean a great deal to me. Except for the fact that my father was away, and I did not like that at all. Nothing in my house, at least not in my presence, was ever mentioned about the plight of Jews in Solingen. I probably would not have understood any of it anyway.

Many books have been written on this subject. By now, the world, has long been introduced to the horror of Nazi Germany and the unforgivable crimes committed against Jews and others during WWII. The world also knows that Jews have been persecuted for centuries, and anything Jewish is subject to discrimination unfortunately even today.

I would be amiss were I not to mention the plight of at least three Jewish families living in Solingen at that time. The following information has been researched by Professor Sassin at a Gymnasium in Solingen. The professor was kind to send me the material, and I am very grateful. I did not know any of these families personally, neither did my family.

The Giesenows

Georg and Jenny Giesenow lived in Solingen. The Giesenows owned and operated a textile store, which opened in February of 1896. Georg and Jenny were members of a local Synagogue. A daughter was born in February of 1898, they named her Else. A son, called Carl, followed in January of 1900. Both children attended High Schools in Solingen. Due to unforeseen circumstances, the family's business had to downsize and moved the store to a different location. Georg was drafted into the military when WWI was raging in 1915.

In later years, daughter Else married and moved to a different city in Germany. Her brother Carl, who had suffered from a lung ailment, succumbed to his illness and died in April of 1922.

The Giesenows were prominent citizens in Solingen, active in numerous organization. But starting in 1933 life became more and more difficult for the family. In the ensuing years edicts were issued prohibiting citizens to purchase any wares from Jewish owned businesses, and on November 9, 1938 a national pogrom, known as Kristallnacht, was ordered by the regime. In that night, the Giesenow's residence and store were ransacked. Georg was arrested on trumped up charges and spent several days in the local jail. His store closed December 31, 1938.

Relatives and friends of the family were fleeing to neighboring countries. Daughter Else, her husband Felix and their daughter Carola had moved some years ago to a city in the Ruhr valley not far from Solingen. Else and Felix sent their daughter with a children's transport to Belgium, hoping to establish a safe haven for the child in that country. Else and Felix followed soon after. In Belgium, they tried in vain to acquire emigration permits for Else' parents.

More trouble befell the Giesenows back in Solingen. Late in the summer of 1939 the Nazis authored a new law, which allowed landlords who rented to Jews to alter the leases. The landlords were now allowed to house a larger number of Jewish occupants to any given residence. A number of Jews were added to the Giesenows apartment, making life even more difficult for the family.

Georg spent his days acting as head of an agency overseeing gathering numbers and statistics of Jews in Solingen. This agency had been formed by the Nazis country-wide to ascertain numbers and residences of Jews in Germany. The Nazis kept meticulous records.

Things went from bad to worse, Jews were being deported in record numbers. The Giesenows spent their last evening in their apartment in Solingen with friends. On the 20th of July 1942, the Giesenows, together with other Jews from the area, were loaded into cattle cars and were deported to the East. The transport arrived in the Theresienstadt concentration camp on July 22nd. Due to extremely inhumane conditions in the camp, six Solinger citizens died even before the beginning of winter 1942. On April 19, 1943, Georg died and on May 13th of that same year Jenny died.

Their daughter and her family survived WWII in Belgium. The Giesenow's granddaughter, Carola, lived in Brussels, Belgium.

The Levens

Alexander Leven married Helene Leven (not related) in April of 1900. The Levens lived on Elisenstrasse in the center of the city. They had three daughters, twin girls Wilhelmine and Margarete born in 1901, and Ilse born in 1914.

Helene and her sister Rosalie had opened a children's clothing store a year before Alexander and Helene were married. The store was located in one of Solingen's busiest commerce areas and was in operation until 1926.

While Helene and Rosalie ran the clothing store, Alexander Leven worked as representative for a razor blade manufacturer. In 1916, he was drafted by the German Wehrmacht (military), from which he was discharged soon after due to illness.

Inflation forced the family to try to survive by doing menial work at their home. Starting in September of 1926 Alexander again found employment as a factory sales representative. After closing the children's clothing store, Helene now found employment elsewhere, working as manager in a lingerie store.

In the meantime, the Leven's children were growing up. Margarete studied at a conservatory in Cologne and worked as a piano teacher. Her twin sister Wilhelmina did not fare as well. She fell ill with tuberculosis and spent one month a year in a sanatorium which specialized in the treatment of people suffering from lung disease. After six years of treatment she was healed. In 1927 Wilhelmina started employment as secretary in a cutlery manufacturing plant. In her free time, she often played the organ in the synagogue until its destruction in 1938 in the Kristallnacht.

Ilse, the twin's younger sister, entered an apprenticeship in the same company where her sister worked as secretary to the Chief Executive Officer.

In 1933 the company was forced by the Nazi regime to discharge all Jewish workers. Ilse found employment with a shoe accessories manufacturer. Her employer was a devout anti-Nazi. He too was forced to discharge any Jewish workers. Margarete lost her position as piano teacher. She and her younger sister Ilse moved to Duesseldorf, a larger city in the Rhineland. Ilse found employment with a Jewish company, and Margarete worked as a sales representative in the same town. Here Margarete met her future husband, Herbert Tichauer. In 1935 the couple emigrated to the Netherlands (Holland).

On April 16, 1938, Alexander Leven, the girl's father, died in a Jewish hospital of pneumonia. He was interred in the Jewish cemetery in Solingen.

One year after her husband's death, Helene Levin emigrated to Amsterdam in the Netherlands to be near her daughter Margarete.

The youngest daughter Ilse was arrested and spent one night in prison in Solingen. The Gestapo interrogated her about her employer, whose company was supposed to have shipped machinery to England. She was released, and a few days later, June 5, she emigrated via the Netherlands to England. During her stop-over in Amsterdam she saw her mother and sister Margarete the last time.

February 23, 1943 Margarete Tichauer, her husband Herbert and her mother Helene were being deported to an interim camp in the North of Holland. From there they were moved to Sobibor and Auschwitz concentration camps and were killed.

Wilhelmina, who re-trained as nurse in 1939 and was living in a neighboring town, was deported to Theresienstadt concentration camp on July 20, 1942. She worked as a nurse in the camp and survived. After her release from Theresienstadt at the end of WWII she moved to Switzerland. She died April 10, 1971 in Zurich.

Ilse, the youngest Levin daughter, had made her way to England, worked as a nanny first, then was employed in various positions for several companies. She married Adrian Shindel, a former resident of Dresden in Germany. Ilse worked many years as translator and secretary for the London-based Baeck Institute. Ilse Shindel died September 2, 2003.

Dr. Alexander Coppel, Esquire

Dr. Alexander Coppel was born in Solingen on September 18, 1865. He was the youngest son of an honorary citizen of Solingen, Gustav Coppel. Gustav Coppel died in 1914.

Dr. Coppel became a lawyer in 1896. At that time, he joined his grandfather's business, a steel manufacturing company. During his tenure in his grandfather's factory, just as his parents had done before him, the grandson was eager to oversee the well-being of the employees. He became curator of the Coppel Institute, which his parents had founded in 1912. In honor of the company's 100th business anniversary, the firm donated two Million Marks for diverse social endeavors in Solingen.

Dr. Coppel held several important positions in the town, one of which was chair of the Solinger Synagogue Community.

But although the Coppel family made major contributions to their hometown in various ways, the family, nevertheless was hounded by the Nazis. Dr. Coppel's sister-in-law, Sophie, emigrated to Switzerland in 1934 with her son, Heinz and his family. It is assumed that Sophie was aware of the persecution of Jews and saw the handwriting on the wall.

In 1936 the Coppel company was "arianized". On the first of March of that year the company was fused with the Kronprinz company, another steel magnate in Solingen at that time.

On April sixteenth, the Solinger plant is taken over by "Arian" management. Alexander Coppel's older brother, Carl Gustav, who lived in Duesseldorf, took his own life on September 25, 1941. Carl Gustav's daughter, Anna, died in 1942 in the concentration camp Ravensbrueck.

In November 1938, Dr. Alexander Coppel was forced by the regime to adopt the first name of Gideon. In 1941, he is commissioned to the downgraded Solingen Office of the Synagogue as community go-between. This office was overseen by the Gestapo headquartered in Cologne. The Cologne office was the headquarter for the Unification of Jews.

In July of 1942, Dr. Coppel was informed that he was to be deported to Theresinstadt Concentration Camp. The following was written by Dr. Coppel to his great-nephew Carl Anton Reiche:

"I am being delegated to the transport to Theresienstadt in Bohemia on Monday, the 20th of July. I never considered the possibility that I, before my death, should have to leave the place of my happiness, in which my parents resided since their wedding day in 1856, and where I was born. This place was my sanctuary. I am walking a difficult road, but I know my God, in whom I trust, will not leave me. That makes me strong. I have enjoyed a rich and beautiful life. It was the joy in my work and in everything beautiful, and there is no doubt that the good name of our house, even today, is valuable. I have been able to assist untold good people, as well as needy people and have been able to continue and deepen my endeavors even until today. That gives me solace...."

On July 21, 1942, Dr. Alexander Coppel, together with other Jews from Solingen was deported to Theresienstadt. Only two weeks after his deportation, on August 5, 1942, Dr. Alexander Coppel died of hunger and general weakness.

Another prisoner, Dr. Emil Kronenberg of Solingen wrote about the last days of Dr. Coppel:

"In July of 1942, Dr. Coppel came to Theresienstadt, just like all the others, without a penny to his name, only with the most necessary clothing. He had to sleep in an attic on a bed of straw. After two weeks, in the morning on his way to the well to wash himself, Dr. Coppel collapsed and died. He died of hunger and weakness. His remains were burned. His ashes, together with the ashes of other prisoners, were placed in a cardboard box and were dumped into the river Eger."

These are only three families of many who had to endure such unimaginable terror. They lived in their, and my, beloved hometown, Solingen. It fills me with a deep sense of shame and sorrow to know that even in this relatively small town inexplicable cruelties were committed to people for no other reason than to have been born a Jew.

For a brief time in early 1938, my parents and I lived in an apartment on Elisenstrasse, just a few houses away from the Leven family.

Unthinkable cruelty was committed by those German people who adhered to the Nazi creed. As far as I know my family was unaware of the horrific deeds of the Nazi regime.

Chapter 1

My maternal grandparents played a most important role in my life. Almost from the moment I came into this world I lived in my grandparents' house. I stayed with them until my fourteenth birthday. I did not know my paternal grandfather, he died when I was too young to remember him. My paternal grandmother was a wonderful woman, but since I grew up with my mother's parents, I did not have a chance to get to know her better. She also passed away when I was quite young. I did visit this kind lady on occasion accompanied by my mother.

In those days cars were not owned by the majority of citizens, so a ride to my father's house to visit my grand mama was always accomplished by a streetcar ride. More of that later.

My maternal grandfather's birth was rather mysterious. The circumstances of his birth were not spoken about in our family. His mother was the local midwife in the small Silesian town of Rosenberg. At that time Rosenberg belonged to Germany, today ownership has returned to Poland. The change-over happened after WWII. Centuries ago it was not unusual for Germany to assimilate various countries into the German homeland, mostly accomplished by war or royal marriages of convenience.

Whenever I asked about my great-grandfather, my questions were answered with silence. My grandmother told me never to approach that topic in my grandfather's presence. That naturally peaked my curiosity even more. The topic was especially fascinating to me because I was never even allowed to mention his name.

I thought my great-grandmother would be easily approachable. She lived in a town close to Solingen, and every so often my grandfather and I would take the train to visit her.

But try as hard as I might, the topic of my great-grandfather was taboo. Since I could not get any answers from my immediate family, I sought out other sources to get the information I wanted. In this case the source was my beloved aunt Hedwig, my grandfather's half-sister.

Aunt Hedwig, or as we referred to her Tante Hedel, was a sweet, unassuming spinster, who in the eyes of the rest of the family had only one flaw, she loved to talk, incessantly. Never anything derogatory about people, but everything else was fair game to my aunt. I loved to listen to her, surprising for a child who had difficulties sitting still any other time. Aunt Hedwig was a walking encyclopedia, especially in matters of faith. She was a devout Catholic, never married. She devoted her life to her beloved mother and the Virgin Mary. I never understood why this beloved aunt did not join a convent. She lived with my great-grandmother and her sister Mia.

With her affinity for the spoken word I deduced that she would be the one reservoir for family history that could be tapped, especially concerning the before mentioned elusive great-grandfather. I was correct.

One evening, I was about twelve at the time, when the rest of the family was busy with other things, I cornered Aunt Hedwig. Since she was of small stature it was not difficult for me to gently push her into a corner of the living room in my grandparents' apartment and deposit her into an easy chair. I grabbed a hassock and sat by her feet anticipating all the news she would hopefully divulge.

At first, I approached the subject gently, then I became more adamant. And so the story was finally told.

My great-grandfather apparently was a Russian General in the Czarist Army, who, so she related, lived to be one hundred and ten years old. I did not believe her at first, to a child one hundred and ten years of age was simply impossible. But I remembered how honest this dear aunt had always been, so I accepted her story. She did not know the General's name, but she knew he was a Russian Aristocrat. Those were the facts as she knew them. That was not enough information for me, I had to know why this person could not be talked about in my family. My aunt answered that all this secrecy was to protect her mother's reputation. Now I was even more than intrigued.

"What is a reputation?" I asked her.

Aunt Hedwig swore me to secrecy and then told me the rest of the story. Apparently, in the late 1800s reputation was a very important commodity, and a woman's good reputation almost always assured her a good marriage proposal.

The General visited Rosenberg with his regiment, met my great-grandmother, who according to my aunt, was a beautiful young woman. The General and my great-grandmother became too close, and her reputation was gone. She found herself to be with child, the General and his regiment returned to Russia not ever having any knowledge of her predicament. I would imagine he probably would not have cared much anyway.

My grandfather was born in a neighboring town, I would think to protect my great-grandmother from wagging tongues. So the poor little midwife was left to raise her boy alone. She gave him a last name, I do not know whether that was her maiden name or the name of the Russian. Unfortunately, I never bothered to ask my aunt. My great-grandmother later married, and aunt Hedwig and aunt Mia were born.

All this secrecy was extremely frustrating, but there was apparently nothing else to be gleaned, and since the other members of my family did not want to divulge what they knew about this sordid affair, I had to put an end to my quest searching for my unidentifiable great-grandfather.

My great-grandmother, aunt Hedwig and her sister Mia and Mia's daughter Susie escaped Rosenberg at the end of WWII fleeing from advancing Russian troops. They found refuge in Radevormwald, a town just a short train-ride's distance from Solingen. Aunt Hedwig would visit my grandparent's house frequently, she loved to be near her older half-brother August, my grandfather. She would arrive without fanfare and unexpectedly, stay a week or so to my great joy, then leave as unceremoniously as she had arrived. I loved that dear woman. During her stay, I would often sit with her and listen to stories of the Bible. I think she had them all memorized.

My maternal grandmother's history was much easier to research. Her grandmother was an opera singer in Holland, and bequeathed her wonderful soprano voice to my grandmother. I was told repeatedly by my mother that my grandmother could hit the high "C" on the scale with ease. At that time, I had no idea what that meant, but I did love to listen to my grandmother singing.

My grandmother was born in Remscheid, also not far from Solingen to a well-to do family. She was the oldest of four siblings, two brothers and a sister. My grandmother was born jaundiced and was not expected to live. Well, thank God she lived, but all her life her skin color was a brown-yellowish tone. She had to be selective about the foods she would eat, her liver did not appreciate fatty foods. She died at age 64 of liver cirrhosis. She never drank any alcohol.

My grandparents met in Solingen. My grandfather had left his home town of Rosenberg long before WWII was raging. He opened a barber shop with an annexed beauty shop and became well established in Solingen in a short while. He had mastered his craft by absolving a three-year apprenticeship, after that five years of journeyman, after which he was able to complete his masters. In Germany, a barber had to go through all this rigorous training, because without that degree he would not otherwise have been allowed to own and run a barber/beauty shop.

My grandmother had been enrolled in a hotel kitchen and entered an apprenticeship to train to become a chef. She had no expectations of ever getting married, so that she insisted her parents allowed her to learn a trade. My great-grandparents reasoned that it was not the worst fate for a young woman to go through life unwed, and learning how to cook would keep their daughter always well fed.

My grandmother was a feisty little thing. Always gentle and kind, but acutely aware of the fact that she was the "runt of the litter" and was made to feel that position in her family mercilessly by her siblings. She had hurdles to overcome and was not well a lot of the time. If she was tempted to eat any kind of food with a high fat content, she would suffer for days. Her liver was her nemesis. But as you will see later, she was one of the bravest and kindest women I have ever met.

My grandmother's favorite food was potato salad which was always prepared by her mother with much mayonnaise. Knowing that her daughter was not able to have this food without having great discomfort, my great-grandmother would prepare a special meal for my grandmother, something she knew my grandmother would like and could eat without any problems. But somehow my determined grandmother would find the forbidden food, ate some of it without her mother's knowledge, and promptly became ill. Her mother often wondered how this happened. She had been so vigilant in preparing "safe" foods for her daughter, but she never found out the reason for her child's malaise, even though a portion of potato salad was missing and none of the family members admitted to the raid on the bowl with the potato salad.

While working in the hotel kitchen she often suffered great pain at the hand of the head chef. Once, she told me, the chef threw a cast iron skillet at her when she had inadvertently not followed the chef's instructions. Another time she felt his wrath in the form of a heavy ladle landing on her back. There were other such incidents but most apprentices knew what to expect, and bore these temper outbursts from the head chef with more or less complaining. Some apprentices left the program early for fear the chef would actually injure them. That, of course, never happened, it was just part of the learning experience.

My grandmother completed her time in the kitchen and became a chef, and her entire family benefited from her schooling. She had not changed her attitude toward marriage and motherhood. She just was not ready to become someone's wife. A true Renaissance woman.

My grandparents met at a community dance. Neither one knew how to dance and did not like the whole thing anyway. But it was a way to get young people together, and my grandparents sat together the entire evening, with chaperones in attendance, of course.

They met a few more times at various functions, and my grandmother realized that my grandfather was getting serious in pursuing her. She liked him, sort of, but was not ready for a serious relationship. She told me when I was older that she found life as a barber's wife too tedious. She just knew he would have residue in the form of tiny hairs all over his clothes, and she was not prepared to deal with that.

Time went on, and then came the day when my grandmother decided it was better not to see my grandfather any longer, and one day she told him so.

She had prepared a little speech, gentle words, to ease the pain that would surely follow. When she was finished, she found my grandfather extremely despondent, and she became frightened. She told him she would think about the whole thing for a few days and let him know, hoping that time would allow the inevitable to sink in.

She would not see my grandfather for a week. Then, one afternoon a very hopeful young man appeared at her house with an enormous bouquet of flowers and proposed to my grandmother. To his great surprise she accepted, and they were married.

I don't know what changed her mind, she never said. I think she may have felt a little sorry for him. To this day I do not think that was the most romantic beginning for two young people. However, in all the years I lived with my grandparents I have never seen them angry with each other. They were happy and content together with the life they had chosen.

When my mother, Inge, was born in August of 1918 times were difficult. WWI had ended with Germany's surrender, unemployment weighed heavily on the nation that was trying to recover from the conflict. Many families had lost their sons and father's and husbands on the battlefield, and the whole nation was in mourning.

Even so, my grandparents were blissfully happy about the birth of their first child. She was a beautiful baby, and her parents doted on her. Seven years later a second daughter was born, my aunt Christl.

Anecdotally I know that my grandparents lived a comfortable life. They entertained frequently, and I heard bits and pieces about wonderful parties in their house. They traveled frequently to my grandfather's hometown of Rosenberg in the Upper Silesia region.

My great-grandmother and her two daughters at that time still lived in the same house in which my grandfather was raised. Her two daughters, Mia and Hedwig stayed with her. The family was able to dwell in that house until they had to flee from Russian troops toward the end of WWII after the Germans had vacated the region.

After this brief introduction to some of my family members, I will begin to introduce my beloved hometown, Solingen. I hold an unwavering affection for this town, that even my repatriation to the United States of America many years ago cannot extinguish.

Chapter 2

Solingen is a mid-size city located between two larger cities –
Duesseldorf and Cologne. The two larger cities are major centers of
commerce and tourism located in the Rhineland. The Rhine River
originates in the mountains of Switzerland and runs from there to
Germany and Holland and finally empties into the North Sea. I have
always been fascinated watching large barges carrying their loads
from one country to the next, and I have often wished I could be on
one of those big ships, watching the changing countryside from the
decks of these barges.

Solingen lies about halfway between her two larger sisters in the
picturesque Bergische Land (Land of Hills). The town has enjoyed
its own renown in centuries past. In the late middle ages swords of
great quality were forged here, and the well-deserved reputation as a
steel town carries through into modern times. Unfortunately, most of
the old mills are gone and were replaced by large steel factories.
Today Solingen is known for her steel giants such as Henkels and
Wuesthoff to name just two. There are many other such industrial
plants calling Solingen home, all of which are known the world over
for creating exemplary cutlery. Top chefs around the globe use
knives made in Solingen. With all of this industry one might get the
idea that Solingen changed from a medieval romantic town into an
unattractive steel center, but that could be not further from the truth.

Around the turn of the twentieth century the center of Solingen
consisted of eye-catching Patrician homes, which displayed beautiful
intricate architectural details. Then there were the less impressive
"Schieferhaeuschen", small houses which are painted with white
plaster and supported by black wooden beams. The latter houses
were occupied by the working class, but are to this day an intricate
part of Solingen adding to the picturesque ambiance of the town.
There are not many Schiefferhaeuschen left, but here and there we
are reminded of their contribution to Solingen's history. The large,
impressive Patricians commanded attention, with their Victorian and
Edwardian spectacular architectural designs.

Most of the larger buildings were owned by successful merchants, who had their living quarters on the upper floors and their businesses located on the ground floor. These massive buildings had at least three levels, and having the private residence above the business was customary for city dwellers.

There were some large establishments strictly meant for commercial enterprise, such as department stores, banks and theaters. The largest of Solingen's department stores was the "Kaufhof", a business concern which held great meaning for me for many reasons. It was owned by the influential Tietz family. The Kaufhof reserved several floors for their customers, the administrative offices were located on the top floor.

Solingen's renown came from the manufacturing of steel in many forms. There were, however many other commercial concerns located in the area. But in the end Solingen is a steel town.

When one leaves the core of the city and travels about five miles in any direction one would be pleasantly surprised by the beauty of the landscape. Gently rolling hills, lush forests with the darkest evergreens, and centuries old mighty oaks, beeches and chestnut trees would meet the visitor. My favorites were the chestnut trees which displayed their beautiful white "candles" in summertime. A softly flowing river, the Wupper, led the way to a medieval castle high above the little town of Burg. In those days, one had to climb up the steep natural elevation to get to the castle, today there is a chair lift to take tourists up the hill. The castle is still in excellent repair and visitors from all over the world can learn about its illustrious history. Upon entering the castle one stands in the Great Hall with its many coat of arms painted on walls and large murals telling of medieval jousts, weddings and knights going off to fight their battles. Going deeper into the castle one can visit a music room, a dining hall, a kitchen, a chapel and then, going all the way to the top, four turrets which invite the visitor to peruse the lovely countryside in every direction around the castle. There even is a dungeon and the accompanying cemetery. I spent many, many days here, admiring the aristocratic patina covered statues mounted on strong stallions guarding the entrance to Castle Burg.

When one takes a leisurely walk along the many nature trails one can happen upon one of the few original steel mills with their large waterwheels turning by the power of the river. In some of these mills one can even meet a professional grinder using the large turning stone to hone a blade to an ever-sharp edge.

The outskirts of Solingen presented a fairytale atmosphere, upon which the steel magnates dared not intrude.

This was my beloved hometown, and to me it was a small piece of heaven. But upon this beautiful place an evil was thrust that defies description. At the time when I begin my story I was totally oblivious of the horror perpetrated by some citizens of Solingen upon a people who they despised merely because an evil dictator persuaded them to do so.

A group of men with one purpose in mind had begun to assail Germany's neighbors. Over the airwaves one could hear such phrases as "the enemies of the Fatherland are plotting Germany's total annihilation", and "Feind hoert mit" (the enemy is listening), all designed to bring the German people into the camp of Adolf Hitler.

He and his henchmen painted a picture of a "Thousand Year Reich" (a thousand-year empire) to perfection. A land where every German would be prosperous, and every German would be able to hold up his head once more. After the total defeat at the end of WWI, the Germans would be proud again. To that end, so they said, sacrifices would have to be made by every man, woman and even child. The time of depression was over, so they said, and paradise was there for the taking. How wrong these fanatics were would not be realized by the populace until it was too late.

This narrative is not so much about WWII waged by Germany against a large contingent of countries around them and across the oceans, but rather about the ordinary day-to-day life of a little girl and her family, who loved their town and were never involved in Hitler's evil schemes, but who, with so many others, became victims of that malevolent regime as well.

Chapter 3

I was born on January 31, 1938 as the only child of my parents, Werner and Inge, and the only grandchild of my maternal grandparents. Naturally I was totally unaware of the political machinations of the Hitler government, nor did I know anything about the economic hardship the German people experienced at that time. The first years of my life consisted of parents and grandparents lovingly caring for me. I will begin my story in the early days of 1943 since I do not recall anything memorable before then.

My "only child" status was a blissful state of affairs for me, because occupying this lofty position brought its advantages. Holidays such as Christmas and my birthday were celebrated as it behooves an only child, I thought. I freely admit I was pampered, and I considered that the natural state of things. Of course, there were also disadvantages not having any siblings, there was no one to blame for my occasional errors in judgment. I was a free spirit even at that young age and had the inclination for getting into some sort of trouble at least once a day.

At this point I would like to introduce my parents. My father, Werner, was a handsome man, and many ladies in my town would have liked to call him their own.

I remember years later during a visit to Solingen I was approached by a lady who asked me if Werner was my father. When I inquired how she knew me, she said she had seen my picture in the local newspaper and that I looked a lot like my father. We spoke for a few moments and she admitted that she had been madly in love with my father, but that he had been unreachable to her. This was not the first time I heard such stories, and I always found it heartwarming to hear these lovely women talk about my dad in such a kind way. Naturally I understood them, my father, after all, was the most handsome man in the world to me. I had returned from America to visit my mother who had been quite ill for some time. I also had planned to approach the local newspaper to see if they could assist me in finding just one soldier who had returned from the battlefield and had served with and known of my father. My father never returned from the war, and as many children of fallen soldiers it was important for me to get as much information about him as I could. The paper was very helpful and sent a reporter to interview me and take a picture to accompany the article they planned on writing. And my quest to find my father and the photo had been seen by many people.

As long as I can remember my handsome father was my hero. He was over six feet tall, with black wavy hair, beautiful hazel eyes, which always seemed to twinkle every time he saw me. My father had an olive complexion and was blessed with a perfect smile with perfectly white teeth. Add to that his riotous sense of humor, and to me he was entirely irresistible. I am sure many girls feel like that about their fathers.

My parents had been enrolled in the same high school, saw each other from time to time and attended some of the same school functions. Neither one had any serious thoughts about the other until they met at a school dance. My father was invited as an alumnus of the school which my mother still attended. Lightning struck and the two young people were inseparable from then on. My mother was the typical ideal of a young German woman of that time, silky blond hair, lovely blue eyes, a warm smile and a personality to match. She was well liked in our town, and there was no shortage of eligible suitors. But all others had ceased to exist for my mother, my father was her one true love. And after a brief courtship my mother agreed to become his wife.

There was one hurdle to overcome, permission from both parents had to be granted. That was how it was done in those days. Parents were revered and definitely played a role in the lives of their children. So, a short time later my father asked my grandfather for the hand of his daughter. It was granted, and my parents were married in a small church just outside of town with the blessing of both grandparents.

Immediately after the wedding the young couple moved into a fully furnished apartment. The two grandparents had formed a friendly coalition and feathered the young people's nest down to the last fork, knife and spoon. For a while life was blissful, but foreshadowing events would soon interfere with their happiness.

I was born the following year and new responsibilities took over their daily lives. My parents were both employed outside the home, so a way had to be found how to care for the newborn. For a while a nanny was hired, a kind woman who I met again later in my life, and I loved her dearly. She told me I gave her a really strange name "Ruebensuesschen", and that no one knew what it meant. Neither did I, but what child has not made up odd names for the people in their lives. She liked the name, and it stuck. Such a dear!

She also related how I was lying in my crib one day, obviously a little bored because she was in the kitchen busy with preparing my bottle, and no one was paying attention to me. So, I entertained myself with undoing my diaper and painting the wall with the content of it. With my fingers, naturally. She said it took her quite a while to clean me and the mess. And she still liked me!

After a few months in my nanny's care, my mother and her mother decided that it was actually quite natural that my grandmother should take over my care during the day while my parents were away at work. She loved being a grandmother and was more than happy with this arrangement. Nanny would still be utilized for walks in the pram and little outings, but my grandmother took the reins. So, I would stay in my grandparent's house during the day, and after work my mother would take me back to the apartment, where we would wait for my dad to come home. In retrospect, it seems I have waited for my father to return much of my life.

Every day people would listen to the radio where they could hear an evil little man by the name of Goebbels, Hitler's propaganda minister, spewing his poison over the airwaves. Unfortunately, people did not realize at that time how evil this man truly was. His silver-tongued speeches touched the damaged German spirit. People had a difficult time coming to terms with the bitter defeat they had been handed after WWI.

Ranting Goebbels would tell the Germans that their leader, Adolf Hitler, would bring Germany back from the abyss. A lot of Germans were taking in by his rhetoric and sadly, believed every word. Whether at a Hitler youth rally or at a more formal event this man was Germany's Svengali, and the people were spellbound. Hitler's loud and boisterous speeches with his Austrian accent were no match for Goebbels. Although Hitler was "the Fuehrer" and adored by a lot of Germans, Goebbels knew how to manipulate the populace to do his bidding. Hitler surrounded himself with a slew of men who were too willing to follow him to war. A great number of these people were military mavens, extremely well educated at German universities, officers of the highest caliber. To this day I cannot understand how these men born into civilized families could become murderous monsters.

The Germans were excited once more. They were being promised to become the great nation again they thought they should be. Greater even, it would be a Thousand Year Reich. All of this propaganda came over the radio daily, intoxicating, and unfortunately people believed it.

Naturally, I did not know at that moment in the story, what all of this meant. I was happy to be with my parents and my grandparents as a child should be. Childhood – unfortunately in my story childhood was short-lived.

Chapter 4

My mother's father was the proud owner of a well-established barber and beauty shop. The salons were on the ground floor of a three-story house, the barber shop was located in the front of the salon and the beauty salon in the rear of the building.

The house was a perfect example of many of the buildings in the older part of town. It was covered from top to bottom with dark gray slate shingles, even the roof. This house must have had special status in Solingen, because when visiting my home town in later years, to my surprise I found one single photo of my grandfather's house in the archives in Solingen.

Upon entering the house, one stepped into the foyer of the barber shop. This part of the salon was beautifully furnished with a mahogany counter with glass panes under which one could see all the articles of a well-stocked barber shop. Underneath the counter, not visible to the public, my grandmother stored her preserves. My favorites were always the peaches.

Behind the counter reaching from floor to ceiling loomed a large mahogany showcase with more barber/beauty shop accessories. To the left of the foyer one entered the actual barber shop through a French doorway. This was the domain of my grandfather and his barbers.

From the foyer, through a doorway and a small hall turning right one entered the beauty shop. Here on could find all the frilly accoutrements befitting the ladies. This area was always of great interest to me, and I loved the beautiful surrounding.

Adjacent to the beauty salon a hallway led through a door to a sizable kitchen. In the kitchen to the right stood a large comfortable sofa with a heavy oak table in front of it and three chairs around three sides of the table. A huge picture window was facing us as one entered the kitchen allowing light to flood into the room. My grandmother's cupboard took up the entire wall opposite the sofa. On one side sat a large stove.

Next to one end of the cupboard was another door opening to a platform which led down a set of stairs into the basement and in the other direction down a flight of stairs into a courtyard. The separation of the two salons from the kitchen became quite important in coming days.

The inside of the non-business side of the house could be reached through yet another front door from which a long hallway led to a flight of wooden stairs leading to the upstairs living quarters of the family.

There was the living room with a piano in one corner, another sofa, a coffee table in front of it, two easy chairs, a mahogany music cabinet with a gramophone, and in another corner stood my favorite piece of furniture, a beautiful green tiled stove which reached almost to the ceiling. This stove had several open compartments, and in those baked apples were kept warm in winter time. Whenever the aroma of baked apples wafted through the room, I knew Christmas, my favorite holiday was near.

Two large windows above the sofa looking out on the street below supplied daylight. One set of French doors on one wall of the living room next to the stove allowed entrance into my grandparent's bedroom. A large bed occupied the opposing wall ahead, always covered with snow-white linens edged with beautiful hand-tatted Belgian lace. To the left of the bed stood my smaller bed covered with identical linens. My grandmother was of the school that bed linens needed to be white, so they could be washed and bleached, and so always were a testimony of the cleanliness of the lady of the house.

Nightstands and a wardrobe holding our clothing completed the decor. There were two more windows facing the street below. One thing I vividly remember about that bedroom was lying in my bed and looking at the ceiling and the beautiful crown molding and a large medallion in the center. Many nights I dropped off to sleep staring at that medallion with its lovely chandelier attached in the center.

When my mother and I moved back into my grandparent's house, it was decided that I should sleep in this bedroom, and my mother took one of the bedrooms on the third floor, which had been her bedroom before she was married. Her sister Christl still occupied another bedroom on the same floor. The reason for this arrangement was because my mother and her sister rose early to go to work, there was no need to wake me.

There were still more rooms on the second and third floor, usually utilized by visiting family or friends.

The attic above the third floor was always one of my favorite places in the house. A lot of old and dusty boxes, old furniture and various mysterious articles made this an extremely fascinating place for a little girl.

Chapter 5

My grandmother was a fastidious homemaker. To establish a clean, comfortable and cozy home had always been her objective. The family's viewpoint was – she really should not labor as hard as she did every day, but nevertheless, everyone appreciated her efforts.

Ommi (a name given to grandmothers by many German children) was no doubt the soul of our home, and even much later after the war had ended she continued to apply her personal touch albeit to much more humble surroundings. The family, as well as friends and neighbors who came to visit often, loved the warmth and comfort my grandmother was able to provide. As a trained chef, she would often display her baking and cooking talents and never let company go hungry. Our house was never a dull place, laughter and singing could be heard in the salons, and after hours in the living quarters. It was a happy place.

My grandmother's father came to live with us for a little while. Some years before his arrival in our home he had undergone cataract surgery, and due to a botched operation was left blind. My great-grandmother had died, and he was not able to live on his own, so he became part of your immediate family.

He was a gentle giant to this little girl. He was six feet four inches tall and weighed over two hundred pounds. He was a very kind man and loved his great-granddaughter dearly, and I loved him right back. He and I had a daily routine which started around seven o'clock in the morning. I would climb to his second-floor bedroom, knock on the door and listen for his full baritone telling me to enter. I would go to the windows and draw back the heavy curtains to allow daylight to come in. His first words after a hearty "Good Morning", were to ascertain if my grandmother had breakfast ready and especially had she purchased fresh rolls at the bakery. This was said in a rather stern voice, but I was always happy to see a smile accompanying his query. I assured him that everything was ready for him. I would take his pants and shirt off a chair and hand it to him, place his shoes on his feet and guide him to the stairway outside his room. After placing his hand on the railing, we would slowly make our way down the stairs.

Often my grandmother would stand at the bottom of the stairs watching the little scene. Sometimes patrons would come from the beauty shop and stand beside her, and a lot a of kind comments were being made watching the giant and the little girl who was so concerned that no harm would come to her blind great-grandfather. I remember these mornings vividly, and I could not understand why people made such a fuss. After all, we did the same thing every morning.

My wonderful great-grandfather passed away not too long after he came to live with us. Thankfully, he was spared the horrible events that followed shortly after he died.

Chapter 6

After finishing his studies, my father's family decided he should go into some kind of business. But he was not to be tied to a desk somewhere, which would have gone against his free-spirited nature. He loved cars and any kind of vehicle with four wheels from the heaviest truck to a family sedan. He could take them apart and assemble them again to the chagrin of his mother who would have liked to see her son settle down in a more "respectable" position like his older brother, the accountant. That was not my father's idea of fun.

When a local merchant offered him a job driving the company's delivery truck, my father was only too happy to accept. Germany's economy was stagnant at that time, many employers were not hiring. My father decided rather than to wait for a better position and a job he probably would not like very much, to accept the offer. My mother was not too enthused about his choice, but after he explained the necessity of earning a salary and providing for his family she consented. I think she wanted to see him happy no matter what, and if driving a truck added to his happiness, she was going to be content as well. Little did she know that her husband would be driving a truck for another employer in the not so distant future.

My father was drafted by the German Wehrmacht (Army) in November 1940. He was attached to a "Pferdetransportkolonne" which means literally translated "Horse Transport Unit". It had nothing to do with transporting horses, as the name would imply, but rather his job consisted of transporting war ordinances, trucks and tanks to the various battle arenas. At any given time, he could find himself in France, back in Germany, then in Russia in the winter battle of 1941/42 and eventually in Yugoslavia, a country in which he later would contract malaria. He was hospitalized several times for this illness and sent to field hospitals, treated and sent back into battle only three days later.

My grand mama pampered my father, he was her youngest child, making his entrance later in her life. He never took life too seriously, but soon he would learn how serious life really was when confronted

32

by an enemy who did not appreciate having his country assailed by German soldiers.

I do not believe that my father knew of the horrendous misdeeds his government committed, he was now a soldier and as such was obliged to obey orders to drive government trucks to designated destinations.

My father was not a simpleton, far from it, but even with his substantial intellect he was not willing to subscribe evil to his government. Such was the power Hitler's henchmen had over the populace. Later, when I was an adult, my mother would tell me over and over that my father was an honest and decent person, and I believe her. My father was blessed with a great sense of humor which he used at appropriate and sometimes at inappropriate times according to his sister Margarete. More of that later.

Chapter 7

My mother's position as manager in a clothing store did not pay a huge salary. After my father was drafted into the military, she was now faced with the fact that she had to raise her child on her own, at least until the war ended and my father was back home again. She searched for new employment in neighboring Cologne, a much larger city than Solingen with more opportunity to get a well-paying job. She was offered a position with a clothing manufacturer. The only disadvantage was she had to take a train to Cologne daily, about a thirty-minute ride. The salary was better, and she started her new job almost immediately.

As much as my grandmother loved me, I am sure it was a difficult task to care for me. She had a house to run, occasionally she helped out in the salon and she had to supervise a precocious five, almost six-year-old granddaughter. It could not have been easy. But the good woman she was, she mastered it all with a sunny disposition.

I remember the time when a new machine entered the salon. I was in the salon and was asked repeatedly by the beauticians not to bother the patrons. I was not doing that, I thought, the patrons did not seem to be unhappy.

One of the ladies was sitting in a chair. Wires and clamps were attached to her head which originated from this new machine, a contraption that looked to me like a torture instrument. My grandmother had told me what it does, but to me it seemed implausible to sit under that thing being electrocuted only to come out from under it after a while and curls had been produced.

Well, before long I was suffering the same fate. My beloved grandmother obviously wanted to punish me for something I had done or said. I was unceremoniously seated under the helmet, clamps were attached to my hair that had been rolled on special rollers, and the electricity was turned on. I have to say in my grandmother's defense, she sat next to me and held my hand the whole time I was attached to the torture machine.

The explanation for this procedure having been inflicted on my six-year old-head is simple. I was the only female in my family who had good, strong hair, and I was used as a guinea pig. This was not the only time my hair was permanent-ed, although that was later in life. I guess if you are born into that kind of business you have to contribute to its success. Although at six years old to turn me into a poor man's Shirley Temple was not to my liking, and I remember crying on my pillow in my bed that night. My objection was that I was definitely not the Shirley Temple type, too tall and not at all as cute as Ms. Temple. Of course, the beauticians never hurt my hair or me, and all the procedures were always followed by treatments to avert any damage to my hair. My grandmother watched over me with Eagle's eyes to keep me from harm.

The following day, I was sent to school, and because children can be cruel at times, I was mercilessly mocked. When I returned home that afternoon, I went straight into the salon, stomped my feet, and with full voice I declared that I was not returning to school until they had made me "normal" again. One of the beauticians conferred with my grandmother, and it was decided my hair should be chemically straightened, with intermittent treatments, of course. At that time, I did not care what they did to my hair, I would have sat still for hours if necessary to have my "normal" hair again. I was fortunate to have inherited my father's strong hair.

I was in the salon on a Saturday morning, "bothering the patrons", I heard the barbershop doors jingle. I did not pay too much attention, but then I heard my mother in the lobby call out" Werner!"

I ran from the back straight in to my father's arms. Tears of happiness streaming down my face. He held me in his arms as if he never wanted to let me go, and all I could think "my daddy is home, my daddy is home."

Some of the patrons who heard the commotion came out of their chairs, some with curlers in their hair or color dripping all over their aprons to welcome my dad back. He was well liked and known in my hometown.

This was the last time my father would come home, after this furlough I never saw him again.

Chapter 8

After all the patrons were gone my grandfather closed the salon, and we congregated in the kitchen around the table. My father had brought me a gift, a board game, and he was anxious to show me how to play it. The game had little tin soldiers that needed to be moved around the board. At the end of the game there was a small prize, and I won every game. I believe my dear dad let me win, but every time when I was awarded the prize he would tell me what a smart girl I was and how proud he was of me. I sat on his lap until late in the evening, he would not let me go.

While my dad and I were busy moving little soldiers, the adults had a thousand questions. At some time during that evening my mother must have realized that he was looking tired and she decided that I should be taken upstairs to bed and that it was time for everyone to retire.

I did not learn until much later that my father still suffered from the effects of a bout with malaria.

All my protesting was ignored and my dad took me upstairs to bed and tucked me in. After many hugs and kisses, my dad promised he would spend the entire next day with me.

The following two weeks went by in a blur. I did not leave my father's side during the day. My friends who usually came to play with me were forgotten. I refused to attend school, and my parents, after speaking with my teachers, agreed to allow me to stay home for the two weeks my dad was home on furlough. I remember complaining each evening when it was time to go to bed, and only my father's assurance that he would still be there in the morning made bedtime more bearable. Storytelling, normally done by my mother or grandmother, now fell to my dad. I think he enjoyed our father-daughter moments. I certainly did, my dad was my hero, and I loved him very much.

Much too soon his furlough came to an end and his dreaded departure arrived. The morning he was to leave he took me in his arms and held me as if he never wanted to let me go. And that is the last memory I have of my father, none of us would ever see him again.

I was six years old when he left to join his company. I remember crying for days, inconsolable. My mother and grandparents tried to assure me that my dad would be coming home for good, and the war would be over soon. The nation still had a year to fight the war, we did not know that at the time.

For days after my father left I was subdued, sitting behind the counter in the barber shop. I did not want to do much of anything. My mother had returned to her job in Cologne. She also had taken a leave of absence while my father was on furlough.

The news from the battle front was not good. Hitler's propaganda machine tried to make us believe otherwise. The screeching rants of Joseph Goebbels came over the airwaves almost daily, and hearing his grating voice was not pleasant to say the least. I overheard all of it, sitting on my little chair behind the counter. The radio sat in close proximity in the barber shop. I often wondered why my grandfather and his patrons wanted to hear these ramblings. But with the radio being the only source of information, it was one way to get news about the war. I wonder if people knew they were being lied to.

More and more enemy airplanes flew over Germany, at this point our Town was not their destination. Other cities did not fare so well. Larger cities to the north of us were being bombed, and we were all wondering when they would fly over Solingen and release their deadly cargo.

My grandfather's patrons consisted mostly of older men or young soldiers who had been so grievously injured they could not return to fight another day. Sitting behind the counter I heard the men talk about such things, and the stories they told were quite different from the information we heard over the radio. I did not know what to believe, a six-year-old usually is not too familiar with conflicting news. But it was obvious, even to me, that the war was not going as planned.

Chapter 9

I missed my father terribly and only my grandmother's assurance that he would be home again before long made me feel a little better. And as children have a way of dealing with sad events, I was soon occupied with my friends, school and time spent in the salon, bothering not only the ladies but the men as well. I liked listening to my grandfather's patrons. They would speak of the war in terms a child could understand. And all of them told me my father was very brave to fight in this war. That made me proud, even though I preferred to have him home with me. But if my dad fought in this big war it must be the right thing to do.

My grandfather was a hard-working man. He would open the doors of the salons at seven o'clock in the morning and did not close until seven o'clock in the evening. All the years I lived with my grandparents I have never seen him take a day off either because of illness or for a vacation. Even the few times he did not feel well, he still stood on his feet in the barbershop all day serving his patrons.

I adored my grandmother. I could not imagine how any child in the world could have a better grandmother. My Ommi taught me to read and write even before I entered my first year of elementary school. She would read all my favorite fairy tales which were my preferred books. I believe there is no fairy tale I have not heard of or read myself written by the brothers Grimm (my best loved fairy tales), to Bechstein and Hans Christian Andersen, as well as the tales of a Thousand and One Night.

Ommi's grandmother was a renowned opera singer in Holland (the Netherlands), and my grandmother inherited her beautiful soprano voice. She often sang along with the radio that was sitting on a counter in the kitchen, while she prepared delicious meals for us.

Even during those uncertain times, the music did not stop in our house until the horrible events that would occur in the near future. One of my favorite memories is the aroma of the Sunday roast cooking in the oven, while tunes of Tchaikovsky's Nutcracker suite were playing on the radio. The waltz of the flowers is still one of my favorite pieces of music. And to think that the composer did not like this particular work at all.

Chapter 10

Sunday was always special in our house. No patrons waiting in the salons, my mother had returned from her position in Cologne, my aunt Christl came home from her apprenticeship in a neighboring town, and the family spent quality time together.

My aunt Christl's wish to be a beautician entailed a three-year apprenticeship with a master beautician. According to the rules of the beauty business, my grandfather could not supply the venue for Christl to learn her trade, it had to be someone who was not related to our family. After her three years my aunt could then work in my grandfather's salon. The rules were stringent, but the students really learned their craft well, and those were the laws in Germany.

Even though our family had grown smaller, my great-grandfather, the gentle giant had passed away one night peacefully in his sleep, my father was absent fighting in a foreign country, the five of us still tried to have Sunday breakfast together.

Chapter 11

I remember one Sunday morning, my grandparents, my mother, aunt Christl and I were sitting around the table enjoying a leisurely breakfast. The fare was the usual for a German breakfast – crispy rolls, rustic sourdough rye bread, smoked prosciutto ham and an assortment of sliced cheeses, jam and fresh butter along with the obligatory soft-boiled egg, which sat in its own little cup accompanied by a mother-of-pearl teaspoon just right for scooping out the delicious yolk. Even during those hard times my grandmother was able to find all these delicacies at a farm nearby whose owners had been friends of my grandparents for many years.

The adults were discussing the events of the week. Being thoroughly bored I started picking at my rolls, removing the soft inside I did not like and placing it on my mother's plate. She looked at me disapprovingly, but continued her conversation with my grandfather. I really did not care whether Mrs. Baumgarden had changed her hair color from black to blond. I remember thinking "why would she do that, I like her black her". I was a little interested that Mr. Schmidt from down the street was growing a mustache and my grandfather had to wax it, up to then I had thought only floors needed waxing. But then something changed, and I felt an uneasy tension in the conversation.

"Mutti", my mother addressed my grandmother, "did you hear the commotion last night? I had just dropped off to sleep, when I was awakened by a noise. It sounded as if men were yelling loudly at someone, but I cannot be sure. The commotion stopped soon after, and I went back to sleep."

"Yes, Inge, I heard them also, it must have been around eleven or so when I became aware of something coming from down the street. It sounded like a lot of shouting. Dad also woke up but decided it was better not to interfere. Since it was Saturday night, I thought some drunken hooligans had come out of the bar at the corner. Who knows what it was, your father was right, it's best to stay out of things that are none of our business. Every day you hear of people fighting and arguing about something, a lot of times about the war. And we cannot change it. Folks are on edge in these uncertain times, and one never knows what..."

My grandfather interrupted her, nodding in my direction adding, "little pots have large ears," which must have meant the topic was not suitable for me.

"Oppi, I am not a pot, and my ears are not large", I said thoroughly dismayed.

"No, child, your Oppi is just joking, you are not a pot, and I love your little ears, and we love you very much. But some things are better left for the adults to discuss." With that I was appeased.

My grandmother continued, spooning out some egg yolk, "it was probably nothing anyway. These rowdies always come home late with too much beer in them to keep the peace." The conversation turned to other topics.

"Vati, were there sirens over Solingen yesterday, "my mother asked. "We heard sirens in Cologne, and everyone in the company was ordered to go to the basement. It was always so stuffy down there, I couldn't stand it and went back upstairs and waited until the others returned. I was reprimanded but I was willing to live with that. There were no planes overhead though, I think they are scaring people way too much with all this constant siren noise."

"No, Inge, there were no sirens in Solingen yesterday," he answered, "but you should have stayed in the basement, child."

When the subject was changed again, I decided not to ask my mother and wait until later when I would be able to ask her about going into someone's basement and why.

My mother then told the family of her plan to visit my father's mother.

"I will take the child to Emma today. I told you that she broke her hip in that fall, and has not been able to leave her bed ever since. The

43

doctors want her to have surgery, but she refuses. She misses seeing Ursula, and the child really should have more contact with her other grand mama. Emma says every time she sees Ursula she reminds her so much of Werner. He always has been her favorite, and in her mind that man can do no wrong," my mother said smilingly. Maybe she knew different.

Chapter 12

My father's mother lived a streetcar ride away from our house, and I remember visiting my grand mama vividly. I do remember that she was a sweet, gentle lady. I have one photo of her with my oldest cousin, Helga and my cousin Wolf and me. But I was too small to remember when that picture was taken. I did know that my grand mama had had a fall and was from then on bedridden until the day she died, long before the war actually came to Solingen. My mother often told me that my grand mama prayed for the return of my father, and said that she hoped to be able to stay alive until my father returned home from the war. It was not to be.

My grand mama lived in a large house, one of those Patrician homes in Solingen of which I spoke earlier in this book. It had three floors, an attic, and a basement with the very necessary "Waschkueche" (wash kitchen). I do not know why that name was given to this place in the basement, it certainly was not a kitchen. A huge stone kettle with a steel liner and a stove underneath it stood in the middle of the room. On washday, the wood in the stove was lit and the water was heated to boiling. The woman (never a man) deposited the family's white laundry in the kettle, and the laundry was boiled for a while. Then she would rinse it in another large vat in clean, cold water, run it through a wringer, the handle of which she had to turn laboriously in order to express the water. When that process was completed, the laundry would be taken to the attic four floors up and hanged to dry. In that respect, our lives today are much easier.

Every time we visited my grand mama, I was treated to more stories about my father. I could never get enough of them. My father's sense of humor was mentioned frequently and was not always appreciated by his siblings, a brother and two sisters. Margarete, the older sister was often driven to distraction by her brother's antics, as was his brother Arthur. The younger sister was in my father's camp, she adored her brother Werner.

My aunt Margarete, whose name I was given as my middle name, was a stern lady. She did not appreciate my father keeping late hours as a young man while still living at home. She thought that my father's youthful transgressions worried my grandmother. My grand mama was a widow, and kept a close eye on her brood. I never knew my grandfather, he died shortly after I was born.

Well, one morning, after a long night out, my father stood in front of the mirror in the kitchen and tried to shave his stubble. Why that was taking care of in the kitchen is a riddle to me, there was a perfectly good bathroom for that. While he was shaving, his sister entered the kitchen, and without much ado proceeded to chastise my father once again for missing curfew and being a problem son. She kept going in that vein for several minutes. My father continued shaving, totally unperturbed. When he was finished, he splashed water on his face and rinsed the soap, dried his face and turned around to look at his aggravated sister. And with a smile he said quietly,

"Grete, if you had said all those things to me, I would really have to get upset with you."

With that he gave her a peck on the cheek and walked away laughing.

Chapter 13

As strange as it seems to me now, my maternal grandparents did not own a car. Grocery shopping was done every day, and we walked to the various locations which were all within walking distance for almost everyone living within city limits. I was often sent to purchase groceries for the family. So, weaving through traffic, I would skip over the cobblestones and make my way to the various destinations.

Supermarkets were unheard of in those days, and the mom and pop stores carried all the items the average housewife needed to provide meals for her family. Vegetables and fruits at the green grocer's, meats at the butcher shop and everything else at the little grocery store on Main Street. One of my favorite stores was a particular bakery. A heavenly aroma greeting the customers upon entering the store was enough to make anyone, and especially this little girl, happy. My grandmother's order was always 12 milk Broetchen (a certain kind of rolls), and I often came home with the Broetchens and my lips covered in powdered sugar from the pastry I was given by the owner.

Another store I liked was a little grocery store. I loved watching the owner scoop flour and sugar out of large wooden bins, deposit the dry goods into paper cones and weigh them on a large scale sitting on the counter.

My grandmother had all the confidence in the world in her little five-year-old granddaughter to return with the items she ordered. I always had just enough money, which made me think that my grandmother was a genius. Often, when I reminisce, I think how wonderful it would be if we could bring those simple days back into this busy world in which we live today. All the technical advances cannot bring back the nostalgic charm of that era.

Chapter 14

The closer the war came to our town, the more often we heard sirens. After a while it became an almost daily occurrence, and people were starting to become complacent. Fewer and fewer people ran to the bunker believing that our town was too small to be of importance to the enemy, and the planes would fly to larger venues.

I remember going shopping with my mother, my grandmother needed some kitchen supplies. Apparently, my mother did not have to work that day, it was a weekday, and she was at home. So, we walked the short distance to the grocery store. I was holding my mother's hands for a while, but then began to run ahead of her, a happy child being with her mother. The sirens began to blare and just out of habit my mother took hold of me and we walked a little faster to get to the store. The sound of the sirens became more urgent, we should have gone to the bunker now, but as I said, we lived in a state of denial. The planes were not going to visit us.

We were lucky again that day, after a while the sirens called the after-alarm. Safe for another day.

We made our purchases, and started to leave, but not before I looked longingly at the big glass candy container sitting on the counter, and pestering my mother to give in to her daughter's plea. Of course, she bought a piece of candy and I was satisfied for now.

Without giving the sirens a second thought, we made our way back home. As soon as we had come within eyesight of our house, we saw my grandfather running toward us.

"Did you not hear the sirens, there could have been a raid", he shouted. I had never seen my grandfather in such a state of distress, nor had I heard him shouting before. He grabbed my hand and practically dragged me into the house with my mother following behind. There stood my grandmother, wringing her hands.

I did not understand the world any longer. What was all the commotion about. Nothing happened, the planes did not even come close to us. Well, the adults were nervous about something that I obviously did not understand. So, I said nothing, followed my grandmother into the kitchen and determined for the time being I would be quiet. But I decided to ask my mother at a later time what a raid was. Not too long after this incident I was to find out what a raid was.

We were to hear many sirens, and trips to the bunker became the norm rather than the exception. I also became familiar with the different sounds of the sirens and their ominous meaning. There was the Vor-Alarm (before alarm) informing the citizens of approaching airplanes, the Hauptalarm (Primary alarm) meaning planes directly overhead and the Nach-Alarm (all clear) when the bombers had left our air space.

I also learned that there were many targets in the area, Solingen was not always the bull's eye. The Bayer Corporation, for instance, not far from our town, Essen in the heart of the Ruhr Valley and the center of Germany's coal industry were also target areas for the allies.

The alarms came mostly at night disturbing our sleep. But as I mentioned we all hoped that we were not the object of our enemy's fury. So even though my grandfather was quite diligent to keep his little flock as safe as possible, he became a little more relaxed, as long as we were all in the house. He would occasionally allow us to stay in bed. He listened to the radio all day long in the salon and at night in the living room or the kitchen, so I guessed he knew when it became too dangerous to stay at home.

Daily activities remained more or less the same. There was an underlying nervousness felt probably by everyone in Solingen, it certainly was present in our family. But life went on.

One day I overheard my grandfather speaking with one of his patrons, "those damned Nazis will not be happy until they have destroyed the whole country."

These kinds of things stayed in my memory because it was highly unusual for my grandfather to use curse words. Who were these Nazis and why did they make my otherwise halcyon grandfather so angry?

I was five years old and I gradually learned that there were really bad things going on around us.

Chapter 15

In the fall of 1943 I was enrolled in Kannenhof elementary school. My first day of pre-school was interesting. Many new friends had to be made and teachers to be met. The schoolyard also needed exploring. And explored, it took a special invitation from sister (catholic nun) to get me to come into the classroom.

I remember I was not too favorably impressed with all the rules and regulation that had to be followed. I was never especially fond of obedience. The time in the schoolyard with all the wonderful equipment made up for all those rules. I was always the first in my class to leave the classroom and the last to come back in, sometimes accompanied by energetic vocals from the teachers.

As a matter of fact, that first day in the schoolyard was such a new adventure that the long-suffering sister had to gently grab me by the scruff to bring me to the classroom. I had to acquiesce, but for the rest of the day I pouted and did not pay much attention to the curriculum.

The end effect of my behavior - a note was given to me with the instruction to return it to sister the next day bearing my mother's signature. I was to learn soon that my free spirit was going to be curbed by a number of nuns devoted to teaching me good manners, patience and devotion to my studies. Unfortunately, those dedicated nuns were not successful in all areas. I did master good manners and some of my studies.

That first day of school was extraordinary in many ways. Upon reading the note from sister, I was scolded when I came home and had one of those unpleasant discussions with my mother that usually entailed some sort of punishment. Thank heaven the punishment was not to be, since other than having been scolded, it was my first day of school and on that day, I received my golden paper cone. German children receive the cone as an award for having advanced from pre-school to first grade. My beautiful paper cone was filled to the brim with candies and chocolates, my picture was taken and the rest of the day was filled with play. My girlfriend, also named Ursula, received her paper cone, and we were allowed to do whatever we wanted, within reason, of course.

In the evening, there was one more surprise, I received a sturdy leather backpack in which I carried my books and pencils. I was now officially a big girl at the ripe old age of five and three-quarter years old.

It could not have been easy for my family to find all these lovely gifts. Many stores had gradually run out of even the most mundane everyday merchandise.

I walked to school daily about one mile distance, and I gradually learned to like my teachers. I was to stay in this school for five years, after which time one graduates to High School. I was absent from this school for one year after the war due to circumstances beyond anyone's control.

Chapter 16

My grandfather had an annoying habit. Every time when we had to take a train to visit friends and relatives who lived further away, he insisted that we be at the train station at least half an hour early. Whether it snowed, rained or the sun shone, he was early and we with him. My grandmother reminded him frequently that the trains always ran on time. No use! That's how it had to be! Many times, I witnessed my grandmother shooting a certain look at my grandfather, but he just smiled, he knew he would always win this battle. In later years my grandmother refused to travel by train with him. I think that is why so many of our far-away relatives came to us, rather than not having contact with my grandmother who everyone loved so dearly.

Today, as an adult, I have the same habit, much to the chagrin of my husband. I just smile knowing that I will win this battle. Some things have a way of repeating themselves.

I have witnessed several times when a train ride was imminent that my grandmother mysteriously developed a terrible migraine. Sometimes she kept me at home with her, which was not to my liking. I loved train rides and did not mind a bit waiting for a train. The depot was already an adventure.

Chapter 17

My first-grade teacher was Sister Assisi, a catholic nun. I soon came to love this gentle soul. During the following year she tried her utmost to control my love for unbridled freedom. I made it difficult for her. Not because I wanted to cause her any grief, rather because I found it unbearably tedious to sit still in class. My report cards, other than showing my basic scholastic achievements, more than once had the handwritten entry that said, "Ursula talks out of turn much too often during class". I found it almost impossible to pay close attention to the curriculum. I especially disliked anything to do with mathematics with all its boring additions, subtractions, and later the difficult to understand algebra. I knew there was a whole world outside the classroom that needed to be discovered. Why did I have to learn mathematics? I am still not good at it.

Sister Assisi often would take me aside outside on the playground, and in her gentle and kind way she would try to explain the finer aspects of behavior, ladylike I recall her calling it. I do not think she believed her efforts would fall on fertile ground. It was not that I purposely tried to be obstinate, there were just too many awesome things to do, rather than to sit still in a classroom listening to lessons that were of little interest to me at that time. Once I realized a few years later that learning was not quite as boring as I thought in first grade, I became much more interested in the subjects. In High School I enjoyed learning languages, as well as history. Math was still not one of my favorites.

Christmas 1943 was not far away. I always liked this holiday even more than my birthday. Usually, Christmas was a time my whole family seemed happier, even I during those ominous days. My only hope in that year was that my dad would come home. That did not happen. Even though we all looked forward to the holidays that Christmas, we were subdued because he was not with us.

This time of the year was also the time when a lot of secrets were being kept by the adults. Naturally this only stoked my curiosity. I looked in any available storage place where my family might have hidden presents. I was a very nosy girl. One day, when I assumed myself to be unobserved, I entered the living room on the second floor. Normally I did not spend much time in that room during the day, but during the Christmastime one never knew where the gifts were hidden. I searched everywhere in the room, and then had the idea that my grandmother might have stashed something under the sofa. So, I crawled on my stomach under the coffee table and halfway under the sofa. The next thing I knew I was being pulled unceremoniously by my ankles out from under the furniture. My grandmother looked at me, shook her head in disbelief and said, "there is nothing hidden in this room, child, now stop all this nosiness or there will not be any presents at all."

That year I promised not to snoop around anymore. I cannot say with total veracity that this promise was kept in years to follow.

My grandmother made this time of the year a wondrous experience. On Christmas Eve, the time of waiting was over, and I was finally allowed to see the living tree standing in all its splendor in our living room on the second floor. Lit wax candles, glistening ornaments in red and gold adorned the tree. We sang the customary hymns, all three verses of all of them, and then it was time for me to go downstairs to the kitchen. The family had decided to display all the wonderful gifts that had been delivered for me in a corner of the kitchen. There just was not enough room in the living room.

That year there was a toy grocery store with many realistic looking packaged food items. There was even a small old-fashioned scale on the counter on which I could weigh the dry goods. Drawers held flower, sugar, dry beans and split peas. Next to the store on a chair sat a life size doll, almost as tall as I was. I loved books, so there were many of them in another corner. I was not able to read all of them yet, but I loved the colorful images on every page. It was truly a rich and wondrous Christmas and the last we would ever spend in my grandparent's beautiful home. The war was about to change everything I had loved and cherished.

Chapter 18

New Year's Eve 1943 was always a big event in my hometown, and it was no different in my family.

Many years later my husband and I spent New Year's Eve 1980 in Solingen, and to this day he says that he had never seen such enthusiasm by ordinary citizens as the people in my hometown displayed.

During the New Year Eve festivities, the hills seemed to be alive with fireworks, not sponsored by the city fathers, but set off by the citizenry of Solingen. All kind of folks took to the street shouting "Prosit Neujahr" (a toast to the New Year) to each other. Even though everyone knew that the war was raging they were still happy to welcome the New Year. Had we known what was in store for us in the new year, we probably would not have been this exuberant.

That day into late evening my grandparent's house was filled with streamers and confetti. There even were bottles of Champagne to be uncorked at the sound of twelve midnight. The food consisted of potato salad (as only my Ommi could make it), bratwursts, hard-boiled eggs, hot dogs and sandwiches.

Friends who had been invited enjoyed every bit of it.

That was a happy evening, and I was allowed to stay up until midnight to greet the New Year with everyone.

Chapter 19

When the holidays were over I again took up my little excursions into the neighborhood as I had so many times before.

"Ommi, can I go and play with Gabi," I asked my grandmother. I had many friends, and Gabi lived just three houses down from ours. It was almost a daily occurrence that after school we would spend time at each other's houses. It was late afternoon, around four o'clock but still light enough to get some play time in.

"Alright, but be back in an hour. Ask Gabi's mother to tell you when an hour is over," my grandmother said.

I promised, put on my heavy winter coat and my boots and left through the salon door, waving goodbye to my grandfather. "Not so fast, little lady," my grandfather called after me, "where are you going this late?"

"I am just going to Gabi's house for an hour. Ommi said it's OK. And Gabi's mother will tell me when an hour is over."

My grandfather nodded, smiled and waved good-bye. He probably would have interrogated me further, but his patron's face was covered with foam, and he let me go. My grandfather was always worried about me, I never knew what all the fuss was about. After all, Gabi's house was just a few doors down. Had my grandfather had any foresight of things to come, he would have kept me at home. But who knew?

I must have my father's car-loving gene. Even today I am happy driving our family car, the heavier the traffic the better I like it.

On this particular day, this propensity for wanting to drive a car (or a truck) became quite obvious. To get to Gabi's house and her back door, I had to cross her backyard. And there in Gabi's neighbor's backyard stood a black, shiny big truck, just tempting me to get a little closer. I had seen this truck before and knew it belonged to Gabi's neighbor.

Well, I did not see a soul anywhere around, so I gave in to temptation, and Gabi was forgotten for the moment. As quietly as I could I opened the driver's side door and climbed onto the seat. Now I was sitting behind the steering wheel. I knew I was not supposed to touch anything, and probably should not even have gotten into the truck, but here I was.

"How bad can it be to touch the steering wheel," I thought. So I did. It was difficult to turn the wheel, and my small hands could barely move it. But I turned it back and forth, making noises like "vroom, vroom, vroom". I could not reach the foot pedals, and I had to crane my neck to see over the steering wheel. Then I saw it! A key left in the ignition. I knew you had to turn the key to start the car (I had watched my dad doing just that). I carefully turned the key. The engine howled. The truck sat on a small incline and started to roll. I didn't know how that happened, I certainly did not engage any gears, I was too short.

Well, the truck did not go very far, a brick wall was in its way and it unceremoniously plowed into the wall. No sooner had this event occurred, when the owner of the truck appeared, none too happy.

"What are you doing, you horrible child," he yelled at me. He reached in front of me through the open cab door and turned off the engine. He pulled me out of the truck and dragged me back by my arm the way I had just come. He never said another word, but judging by his curiously red face I ascertained I was in serious trouble. I decided for once to keep quiet.

"August," he called to my grandfather, "guess what that little stinker has done now? She drove my truck into a wall!"

"Well", I thought to myself, "driving definitely was not the right word to use here. I did not drive the truck, it rolled, and only a couple of meters at that."

"Is she alright?"

That was more like it. That truck could have inflicted great bodily harm to my now six-year-old body. And anyway, it was the owner's fault, he should not have left the truck open and the key in the ignition. I was indignant.

After the truck owner had calmed down a bit, and I had apologized for driving his truck and would never do it again, I noticed that the patrons in the salon were smiling. That gave me an inclination that I might be off the hook again.

But this incident made it clear to my mother and my grandparents that I needed to be supervised much more rigidly. I was still allowed to wander around the inner city on my own, but I was not to entertain any driving adventure ever again until I was old enough to get a license. I promised.

Chapter 20

After school and homework, I usually wandered around the city center. I was allowed to do that, but was not allowed to bother business owners. There was an optometrist shop that was of special interest to me. This shop's attraction was an oversized pair of spectacles attached to the eaves of the building right above the storefront window. My grandmother had what I called an affliction, she habitually lost her reading glasses. So, I had an idea how I could remedy my grandmother's troubles. I entered the optometrist shop. I knew I was not to worry merchants, but the way I saw it this was a necessity. I approached the first person I saw, who happened to be the owner.

"What can I do for you little lady," he asked with a smile on his face.

"I came to buy glasses for my grandmother," I said.

And just to show the man I was serious I pulled a small coin purse from my dress pocket and poured its contents on the glass counter. There were twenty-seven Pfennig (pennies) which represented my entire savings.

"Well, that is quite a fortune you have there," the indulgent proprietor said, "and we have a lot of glasses. Which glasses were you thinking of purchasing? Are they for you?"

"No, no," I answered, "I am only six years old and my eyes are not old enough. I can see very well."

At that time, I thought the man was not very smart.

"I want to get glasses for my grandmother, and they have to be very large so she cannot lose them all the time. I saw the big glasses outside your store, and I thought you surely can make a large pair for my Ommi, so she will never lose them again."

I did not know why this man kept smiling at me, I was very serious. My grandmother's lost glasses had become a problem in our house. I was always expected to find them. Well, once in a while I was successful, but most of the time the glasses remained lost. And my grandmother ended up having to buy a new pair.

I remember my Ommi telling me about a bird called a magpie. This bird was attracted to anything shiny. It would steal anything shimmering wherever it could find it, even from windowsills.

So, when the optometrist asked me why my Ommi was misplacing her glasses I answered with childlike reasoning, "I think a magpie steals them."

Well, the man returned my money to me and asked me to sit on a nearby bench and wait for a few minutes.

Before long, my grandmother entered the store. She thanked me for wanting to help her with this problem, and explained that large glasses would not fit on her tiny nose. We left the store with apologies to the owner for taking up his time. He said he enjoyed my visit with a twinkle in his eyes. I escaped a scolding. After all I was only trying to help my beloved grandmother.

Much later I found out that my grandparents knew the optometrist very well. Many of the merchants in our town were acquainted with each other, and many of them were to get to know me also.

The problem with my grandmother's glasses, however, persisted. I think she must have had a running bill at the optometrist.

Chapter 21

A few days later I visited the Kaiserhof, a local four-star restaurant. This restaurant was about three blocks from my house. It was around the noontime and I was hungry. I knew the owner was a friend of my grandparents, so I decided to see what was cooking. I entered the beautiful dining room, all tables wore snow white table cloths and a little vase with fresh flowers in them. I thought it looked very nice and reminded me of home. I found a table by the window and sat down.

A waiter approached with a curiously friendly smile. I had never seen him before, so why was he smiling at me so broadly? Hmm!

"Would you please bring me a bowl of soup. Do you have pea soup the way my Ommi makes it? And could I also have some of those little pieces of bread in the soup? I like them a lot."

He said he was going to see what the chef had prepared, and before long he returned with a steaming bowl of soup, pea soup with croutons. I was a happy girl. It never occurred to me I might have to pay for the soup. After all, my Ommi and Oppi were friends of the owner, so eating soup here was perfectly normal. And with that I thanked the waiter and was ready to begin my meal.

"Be careful, Ursula," he said, "the soup is very hot."

How did he know my name? I began to think that too many people in my hometown knew my name. Well., I got around a lot. Before the waiter let me start spooning my soup, he placed a white napkin on my lap.

"That's not where my Ommi puts it, it goes under my chin."

But I thought it was better not to interfere. I think I was a bit intimidated by his black suit and bow tie. No one I knew wore those.

So, I finally ate my soup, making sure I did not spill any of it. Looking around at the other diners, I noticed people were also smiling at me. It must have been a special day with all that smiling going on. I believed it was because Solingen was a friendly town.

A short time later, the door opened and my beleaguered grandmother entered the restaurant. She seemed flustered. I was happy to see her, of course, but how did she know where to find me?

The owner, seeing my grandmother, came to meet her. And with assurances of the owner that no one thought that my family did not feed me enough, my grandmother and I left the restaurant. I believe my grandmother offered to pay for the soup, but that was declined, as I knew it would be. But my Ommi was not amused.

"What goes on in that head of yours, child, you cannot just go into places, try to buy eyeglasses, then go to the restaurant and ask to be fed. It is embarrassing to your grandfather and me. People will think we let you run around wildly and that we don't take good care of you."

I had never seen my grandmother angry before, and I did not want to see that again. I promised myself never to embarrass my Ommi again, even though I did not think I had done anything wrong. I did not tell that to my Ommi.

My grandmother forgave me again, and I felt much better.

Chapter 22

My school days in 1943 were relatively uneventful. Although there was that time when Sister Assisi decided that the whole class should go on a field trip. Sister could not accompany us due encroaching age and bad knees. I asked her if that was from too much kneeling. She assured me that she was very old, and that knees naturally wear out. But that kneeling was very good exercise for the soul. I did not understand that then.

A substitute teacher was assigned to lead the class on this fun trip through the countryside.

We were all very excited and a lot of hollering was heard, something that normally was not allowed in the classroom. What a great idea of Sister, I thought, to allow the whole class to get away from the grind of scholastics. No math, no sitting still, and I would not hear the dreaded words "Ursula, stop talking!"

We lined up in rows of three in the schoolyard. Everyone was to hold hands, and Sister admonished us to listen to the teacher. We promised. The school had its own transportation, an outdated bus that had seen better days. But to us it was beautiful. The driver had been the caretaker at the school for many years and was well trusted to take his precious cargo to the destination. I do not remember how many children we were at that time, but we made enough noise to wake the dead. It was a perfect day for an outing in the woods. The sun was shining, it was comfortably warm, one of those beautiful late summer days.

Teacher, who sat in the front seat occasionally blew a whistle to calm down all the laughter and talking. It worked for a little while, but our exuberance knew no bounds. I think she understood.

Finally, the bus stopped not far from the forest path we were to take. We jumped off, lined up and marched like little geese, three abreast, teacher in front and the driver in back. The sunlight filtered through the trees, but it was bright enough to see all the wonderful things around us. A little toad here, a praying mantis standing motionless in the grass, butterflies fluttering around and all those wonderful trees, it was nature at its best. We had a great time that day, and we were quite well behaved. A lot of teaching about flora and fauna of the region became our lessons for that day. I remember thinking how nice it would be if we could have lessons outdoors rather than in a stuffy classroom where stale air either made me sneeze or yawn.

We had wandered a while, some of us singing, some only talking to each other, some laughing and just generally enjoying ourselves. I really tried to listen to teacher instructing us in the wonders of nature, but it was difficult for me to pay attention to lessons with all the beautiful things around us.

All of a sudden, we heard teacher shout," quickly children, move along, quickly now and quietly, do not run, just walk forward."

What was the matter? Why was teacher so upset? As instructed, we walked, and as I turned around I saw what had frightened her. A huge snake was coiled around a fence post. The animal was not moving, but as soon as we saw the snake we forgot teacher's words and started running, some children were screaming, I think I was one of them. All we wanted to do was to get away from that beast as fast as our small legs could carry us, until teacher told us we could stop running and we were now safe. We made our way back to the street, out of the forest and to the bus parked on the street.

It had been a wonderful day, even though it had to stop abruptly. I believe teacher was too upset to continue our walk. The snake really frightened all of us, and I was happy that the reptile decided to stay on the fence post. Maybe it was digesting.

I grew up to love animals of all kind, except snakes. My husband has urged me to touch a snake here and there when the opportunity arose to do that, and I have given in and touched them. But I am still not a friend of snakes. I will never have one as a pet, I stick to dogs, cats and horses.

Chapter 23

World War II had now been raging for some years, and the battlefield seemed to get closer to my beloved Solingen. I don't know if my family actually knew the extent to which the regime had taken the conflict, it was never spoken of in my presence. And except for the few snippets I overheard spoken by my grandfather's patrons, I was blissfully unaware. I believe that my family tried diligently to keep the war as far away from me as possible. However, there soon came a time when all their attempts at keeping me protected came to an end.

As a now six-year-old every day I realized things were not the same. I knew there were soldiers who were sent to fight this war in far-away places, as my father did. We saw soldiers in the streets of Solingen more often, men who were walking with canes or sitting in wheelchairs. Some had empty suit sleeves or pant legs which were pinned up to prevent them from flying around loosely. I remember feeling extremely sad when I saw these once strong and healthy young men, and I prayed fervently that this fate would not befall my beloved dad.

Up to now, Solingen had been unscathed, except for one raid that inflicted relatively minor damage to the town. However, there was an unease in the air. It was difficult to explain. It was a feeling that something dreadful was coming toward us. In the summer of 1944 we had no idea how really horrible it was going to be.

In our kitchen, next to the beauty salon the radio played all day. I often heard that there apparently was an enemy who wanted to destroy our country and us. Why, I thought. Were we not nice people? My family never hurt anyone, so why was there an enemy, and how did he become our enemy? Did we do something so horrible that we needed to be destroyed? And what was that? It was a confusing time for a child who did not understand the reasons for this terrible war. But I thought if my dad was fighting in this war, he would keep all enemies away from us. I was so naive.

When I allow my mind to drift back to those years, (an exercise I do not often employ), one emotion invariably comes to mind. Uneasiness! It did not have an origin in something concrete, because I still thought the war would be over soon, my dad would return and all was going to be well. But there was a feeling of foreboding that something was about to happen. You could see this uneasiness in people's faces, even in the way they spoke. Smiles were largely absent, and conversations would soon turn to the war.

With my unquenchable optimism, I searched every day for pleasant and non-threatening ways to spend my time. I spent a lot of time with my friends, and war was a topic was not allowed. We would busy ourselves playing games, taking our doll babies for strolls in their prams, and the only thing missing was a dog. I wanted a puppy so badly, but my grandmother did not succumb to my pleas. She said a dog was a big responsibility, and she did not have time to watch one. I guess, during that uncertain time, a dog was probably not a good idea. We had more important things to worry about.

Chapter 24

About one hundred yards distance from our home and down a small hill stood an above ground bomb shelter. The shelter was in the form of a super-size cone, wide at the bottom and narrowing into a point at the top. It stood about 45 feet tall. These type of bomb shelters were called Winkeltuerme loosely translated corner towers. A strange name for a building that did not have one corner on the outside. These shelters began to appear in Germany in 1936. I guess the government had them erected in anticipation of eventual need. The reason for the shape of the shelters was to deny incoming bombs an easy target. These shelters were constructed of huge concrete blocks, each about two feet wide, and meant to give people the safest place during air raids.

A lot of us children who lived in the vicinity of this bunker would play in its shadow daily. It looked a little scary with its impressive height, but when my grandmother told me it was just another building with an odd shape, it was no longer threatening. So Gabi, the other Ursula and I played outside the shelter in the grassy areas, forming wreaths of wildflowers and adorned our heads more or less successfully. We would run up and down the wooden steps leading to the imposing iron doors, or just sit in the shade of the large chestnut tree and relax.

Sometimes the iron doors would open to accommodate the caretaker, an elderly man with a constant twinkle in his eyes, who often would allow us to look around in the bunker. There was a small room to the left of the door just large enough to hold a cot and a chair. This tiny room was lit by an industrial lamp attached to the ceiling with a metal guard around the bulb. I called it 'bulb in a cage". This small space was to become important to me in the very near future.

To the right of the door concrete steps led down to a subterranean room about ten by twelve feet in size. The caretaker kept some of his cleaning materials here. To the right against a wall sat a bench, and on the opposite wall stood tall, round oxygen tanks. That was the extent of the furniture, very sparse, but then no one would want to live down here. I wondered why there was a bench and oxygen bottles.

I asked my grandmother about the oxygen bottles and what they do, and she explained that some people suffer from illnesses and needed extra air to breathe. Maybe the caretaker needed it. I would soon see these oxygen tanks in action, much differently than providing air for the caretaker.

Back up on the first floor in the shelter a seemingly endless flight of spiral stairs led to the top. This bunker was built for strength not for comfort. As much as I loved to play outside the bunker, the inside was not a place in which I wanted to spend too much time.

This shelter no longer exists, it was demolished sometime in the 1950s. During the war years it was considered to be one of the most secure bunkers in Solingen.

My grandfather had been elected to be bunker warden by the town council. Our house was the closest to the shelter and it seemed a logical conclusion. My grandfather was well known in Solingen as an exemplary business man, so I think the city fathers must have known he also would do a good job as bunker warden.

Chapter 25

We had no need of the bunker until later in 1944. The planes primarily stayed away from Solingen until then. But I do remember in the summer of 1943 when a neighboring town, Remscheid, was bombarded heavily, ashes rained on our town for days.

I remember my grandmother crying. I was alarmed and asked her why she was so unhappy, and she told me that she grew up in Remscheid, and that the city had been attacked by enemy bombs.

I was unusually quiet in the following days. I hated seeing my grandmother so sad, and I remember thinking that my beloved Solingen could meet the same fate as my sad grandmother's hometown. Remscheid was not very far away from us.

I asked about my father more than usual. I longed to be held by him, telling me that everything would be alright. I wanted to see his wonderful smile, I wanted him to tell me that he personally would chase the bad guys away. I did not know at that time that I would never see my beloved father again.

Even my quiet grandfather, who at times was more than exasperated by the antics of his unruly granddaughter, became concerned by my unusually calm behavior. So, one day, between patrons, he sat me down in one of the red leather barber chairs and began to ask me questions. What was bothering me, he wanted to know. Was I afraid of anything? Did all the talk about war that I heard from all kind of sources frighten me?

I told him I only wanted my daddy to come back and chase the bad "Tommies" away. And that I did not think my grandfather could help me with that because he was not tall enough.

Children speak what is in their heart and mind. I had not given any thought to the fact that my babble could have hurt my grandfather's feelings. I only knew that my grandfather did not have the strength to chase this horrible enemy away.

My grandfather was an amazing person. He became physically challenged when a childhood accident left him with a permanent and severely curved spine. It was an obvious affliction, in those days it was referred to as "hunchback". He probably was not much taller than five feet and four inches. He must have been in great pain many days, but nevertheless he opened his shop at seven o'clock in the morning, and would be on his feet until late night serving his patrons, cutting hair and shaving beards. I never heard him complain in the fourteen years that I lived with my grandparents.

Later, in the final days of the war, when the regime drafted twelve-year-old boys and men sixty and even seventy years old, my grandfather received a draft notice. He was to report to a military post not far from my hometown. He knew there was no way to refuse the draft, so he reported for duty. He returned to his family after a few weeks, his back would not allow him to take part in the rigors of military life.

When my grandmother saw him coming down our street in his ill-fitting uniform, with tears in her eyes she mumbled to herself, "now we definitely have lost the war." She might have had a sense of foreboding.

So, my grandfather returned to his patrons and also resumed his position as bunker warden. He took that job very seriously, he often said that in times of emergency he was responsible for many lives. He inspected the bunker daily and made sure that the large oxygen bottles were filled to capacity.

During the summer of 1944 the sirens blared more frequently than ever before. We were awakened mostly at night, ran to the shelter, only to hear the sirens telling us that it was over for now. I was tired of all this running and one night I asked my mother why we had to run to the shelter so often. Nothing ever happened, couldn't we just stay at home and not obey the sirens? Why were people trying to hurt us, who were these "Tommies" everyone spoke about? Why were planes flying over our town so many nights and woke us up? Solingen was a beautiful town, why did they want to destroy it? I was done with all of it.

71

I had been listening to too much talk in the barber shop without really understanding, but now I wanted to know. My mother told me that I was too young to comprehend the complexities of war. Well, at almost six and a half years old, I thought I was quite old enough to understand. My mother said that the adults were trying to keep everything that pertained to the war away from me.

I thought that obviously was not working, because all this talk of me being too young to understand was making me more insecure and afraid. If only my dad would be home, I thought, he would explain everything to me. He would not think I was too young.

My mother seemed to be pre-occupied and sad most of the time. It was difficult for her to be away from her child during these unsettled times. She had tried diligently to find employment in Solingen, but had not been successful.

When I asked her why she had to go to Cologne to work, could she not help in the salons? She said she had to make a lot of money to provide food for the two of us. I did not believe her because I knew my Ommi would feed us, and she would not make us pay for our food.

Well, my constant nagging brought its results. I felt extremely proud of myself that I had been able to make my mother see the error of her ways. It was decided that my mother should give up her job in Cologne and help my grandfather in the salons. She had tried her hand at curling ladies' hair and shampooing many times before. Much later she would learn the art of coloring, a discipline in which she would excel.

I was happy she was home with us, and I was very proud of her. Business, however became more and more sporadic. Many women's husbands and fathers were away at war, the ladies were not quite as concerned with their outward appearance. Staying safe during these stressful times was on everybody's mind.

Chapter 26

The war front had gradually encircled the "Reich". Propaganda Minister Joseph Goebbels still screeched his venom over the state-controlled airwaves, urging every German to do his or her utmost best for the Fatherland. He claimed that victory was just around the corner. I do not think many Germans listened to him anymore, they must have wondered if he really believed what he was saying.

Many families in my hometown received letters of condolence from the Ministry of Defense, informing them of the death of their loved ones, and many had lost all hope of a peaceful resolution to the war.

A restful night's sleep became more and more infrequent. My family seemed to be in a constant state of exhaustion. The nightly excursions to the shelter, warranted or not, had taken its toll on all of us.

Then there was the problem of securing food for all of us. But the food part did not concern me as much, because somehow my grandmother was still able to conjure up delicious meals. Lack of sound sleep was a problem. My grandmother told me that often she would find me sitting at the kitchen table fast asleep. I did not even complain when the once hated "nap time" came around.

Most of the days I would busy myself with visits to Gabi and Ursula, and for those hours the war was forgotten. I think we tried to convince ourselves that everything would be well, the government headquarters in Berlin was far away from our town, the front, of which I had heard so much, was in a distant land, and our brave soldiers would keep us all protected.

I noticed changes every day in the summer of 1944. Small things at first proved that not everything was as it had been. Gone were the days when I would ask my grandmother's permission to get a jar of her home canned peaches from under the counter in the lobby. In the past, she often had said no, and directed me to a jar of pears or any other fruit, just not her treasured peaches. They were only meant for

Sundays. But now she allowed her cherished peaches to be opened even during the week. Now I really knew something was wrong.

Many years later I would recall her saying to me," child, I wish I would have let you eat all the peaches."

Gone also were the days when my beloved grandmother and I would take our midday nap together on the comfortable sofa in the kitchen. At that time, she would recite all my favorite childhood stories to entice me to fall asleep. And with her indomitable patience she would tell me the same ones over and over again.

Now I took my nap by myself. Changes had taken place before my eyes, and there did not seem to be a way to bring the good times back. My dear grandmother had changed from the most mellow woman I had ever known to a person who startled at the tiniest noise. She did not want to sit still for any length of time, and it seemed that taking a nap with her granddaughter was not part of her day any longer. I missed my grandmother. I think it was at that time that she started to take her Valerian Root drops on a sugar cube to calm her nerves, she said. I did not know what nerves were or why hers made her so jumpy, up to that time I also did not know that my grandmother had nerves. But whatever they were, the Valerian drops did not help. She was not calm.

Photos of the time period.

My maternal grandparents.

My maternal great grandmother and my mother, age about 14.

My mother and my grandmother.

My parent's wedding day (I don't know what they did to my mother's hair).

My grandfather strolling through Solingen in better days.

My beloved father.

My grandparent's silver wedding anniversary. From left to right -
front row - my grandmother, her father (who was blind), my
mother's cousin Luzie, my mother's sister Christl holding their
cousin Charlotte. Back row - my grandfather, my grandmother's
sister Bertha, my mother and friends,1943.

This was my grandparent's house with barber/beauty shop.

My grandfather (white straw hat), just down the street from his barber shop.

The Kaufhof - the department store in whose ruins my grandmother and I sought shelter from the bombs. The store, as well as all the buildings you see in this photo, were destroyed in November 1944. The bunker was located diagonally left, between two buildings and down a small hill.

A view of one of the streets of Solingen before WWII.

The restaurant where I asked for pea soup.

This picture was taken around the turn of the century. These were
the buildings I saw every day before the war came to Solingen.

Old marketplace before WWII.

My grandmother and I

My grandfather and I.

A visit to my father's mother. My grand mama holding my cousin
Klaus. I, staring at the ceiling, and my cousin Helga in the back row.

My grandfather (front center). When my grandmother saw him in his ill-fitting uniform, she said jokingly: "Now we really have lost the war."

My grandfather and I.

Playing in the sun in front of our bunker. Clearly seen, the wooden steps leading to the iron doors. I played on and around those steps many days.

Proudly holding my first day of school trophy - My candy filled cone!

View of our bunker and surrounding areas after November 1944.
Ruins and burnt out houses all around. The bunker stood unharmed.
It was pockmarked from bomb impacts, but it survived.

This was the view in the vicinity of the bomb shelter.

My once beautiful Solingen - in ruins! The church had lost its steeples.

The street next to our bunker, where the prisoners of war had threatened me.

The demolition of the bunker took place in the 1950s.

The shelter was demolished in the 1950's

From left to right, Doris (a friend) and I holding the veil, my grandfather, Dorothee and Rosemarie (friends). Back row - my mother behind me, her sister Christl, her new husband Bill and Bill's best man, 1950.

Dorothee, friends and I at play. Dorothee facing the camera, my back turned to the camera. To my demise, I was always the tallest.

My grandparents and their "staff "(one beautician) in front of the new beauty shop after the war. My grandfather never recovered completely from the loss of his original shop.

This is the house in which we lived after the war. From right to left - first floor above the shops - window of our bedroom, the dormer with the three windows was our living room. The next dormer was Dorothee's parent's living room and the last window, her parent's bedroom.

My "Ommi" reading her Christmas music in our new house.

Schloss Burg! The castle in the hills around Solingen.

Chapter 27

In the following days and months, I noticed something odd. Some people's heads seemed to be cocked to one side, as if they were listening for something. I had noticed the same in me, I tended to listen to noises from the sky. I guess we were all expecting sirens. Much later, after the war had ended, I still listened for those alarms warning us that enemy planes are flying overhead. I learned to hate the sound of sirens. Even today, when sirens blare in our quiet little town where I live with my husband, I cringe.

I was very happy my mother was with us all the time now. I had worried about my mother and the train rides she had to take that took her so far away from me. Even though I loved my Ommi dearly, I still wanted my mother to be around me. I never understood why my mother had to make all that money to provide for us. After all, my grandfather probably had enough money to take care of all of us while my dad was fighting in the war. It was all too difficult to understand for me. I only knew that sometime soon my dad would make everything normal again. I did not know at that time, nor did any of us, that my father had been captured by Yugoslavian partisans and was held prisoner in a town near Zagreb, Yugoslavia.

As much as possible, I tried to stay out of everyone's way. People were just so tense, I did not want to add to the stress they seemed to experience. So, I stuck to my favorite things to do. I decided to take a little stroll down the streets and lanes of my beloved Solingen. I wanted to see if other people were as nervous about the way things were now as my family seemed to be. First stop - the large department store, the Kaufhof, was just the right venue for my quest.

The Kaufhof had many wonderful things to offer to a little girl. Many of the clerks knew me from previous visits. No frowns or serious faces here. As usual I was greeted with smiles by all the employees. My immediate stop was always the toy department on the first floor. Among many beautiful things displayed there, were dolls, many wonderful dolls. My favorite doll was one with long blond curls and a tiny tiara sitting on her head. She was wearing a pink princess dress and tiny pink slippers.

"Good morning, Ursula. Did you come to see if your favorite doll is still here? I think she will wait for you, don't you?"

The kind lady who managed the toy department knew how to make a little girl happy.

"Yes, I did", I answered, "would it be alright if I held her again for a little while?"

She took the toy from the display and handed her to me. I carefully cradled the doll in my arms, taking care not to wrinkle her lovely dress. As often as I had come to visit, I was always allowed to hold this doll for a few minutes. There was no shortage of dolls at home, but this doll was very special to me.

After exhausting my admiration for my favorite toy, I was allowed to return her to her rightful place on the shelf behind the counter. Years later, while walking to my high school, I passed the Kaufhof every day. And I saw the same kind sales lady almost daily while stopping at the Kaufhof for an ice cream. I did not stop at the toy department very often anymore, but we would wave to each other from across the hall. I will always remember her as the kindest sales lady I had ever known.

Chapter 28

On this particular day, a greater adventure awaited me. After the happy visit in the toy department, I climbed up the wide stairs of the Kaufhof to the second floor. Nothing interesting here for a little girl. Only drab things like clothes and furniture (I have since changed my mind on this subject).

I climbed up the stairs and reached the third floor, a non-familiar area up to that point. I do not remember what made me decide to go up there, I guess I felt adventurous and wanted to see what was above the second floor. No one paid any attention to me. I came to a long hallway at the end of which was a sturdy door. I opened it, at least I tried to open it. The door was too heavy for me. Up to this point I had never encountered a door I could not open. The steel doors in the bomb shelter were heavy also, but they were always opened by the caretaker.

I knocked and knocked, no answer. I kept knocking and probably could have kept knocking without avail had the door not opened from the other side, and I found myself looking up at the most beautiful soldier I had ever seen, except for my father, of course. This one was different though, he looked almost angelic with his blonde hair and steel blue eyes that seemed to smile when he saw me. His uniform looked different from my father's.

"Well, what do we have here," he said, "who allowed you to come up to this floor?"

I was startled and did not know how answer that question. Did I need permission to come up here, I wondered?

"You're not in trouble," he said when he noticed my alarm, "stay right here, I am going to get some water, I will be back in a second, then I will take you to meet a lot of nice soldiers."

I was so excited, I loved soldiers, who were so much like my father. So I promised to stay in place and wait for him. He was as good as his word, and when he returned he took my hand, he opened the door. What I saw beyond that big door I had never seen before.

I found myself on the roof of the Kaufhof. The space was filled with gigantic machinery. In front of those contraptions sat men in uniforms, soldiers all of them.

"Hello, and who are you," one of them asked, "can you tell us your name?"

"My name is Ursula and I am six and a half years old, and I come to the Kaufhof often. What is your name, and what are you doing here?"

By now all the soldiers had noticed me, and I promptly became the center of their attention. These soldiers in their crisp uniforms immediately became my friends, and I theirs. The name of the soldier who had taken me inside was Axel, and he became my special friend.

He picked me up and lifted me on his lap right in front of one of those machines.

I guess I should have been alarmed. Here I was sitting on the lap of a total stranger, sitting in front of war machinery and talking to more perfect strangers. I was not scared in the least. After all, these were German soldiers like my father, I instinctively knew there was no reason to be afraid.

All the soldiers on that roof that day left their positions behind their machines and surrounded me. I was really impressed.

"So, tell us, Ursula, where do you live and what brought you to the roof?"

"My grandfather has a barbershop just across the street, and I live there with my grandparents and my mother and my aunt Christl. My father would live with us, but he is a soldier, too, and he is at the front. You know, that's where the war is. That's what my mother always tells me. She never tells me where the front is, though. Can you tell me? Is it far from here, the front I mean? I really miss him a lot, and I pray all the time for him to come home soon."

I noticed the men looking at each other, and Axel hugged me and stroked my hair, as if to tell me it's going to be alright little girl.

"We will pray for your dad to come home soon, as well," he said. Now I knew my dad would come home with all that praying going on. Axel continued to hold me in his arms, and I was happy to stay on his lap. I felt very safe there.

After a while all the men told me their names, there must have been ten or twelve soldiers. I do not remember the names any longer, except Axel. But I have wondered many times over the years if these soldiers ever came home to their families after the war. I hope they did.

Still sitting on Axel's lap, I was now no longer content to just be hugged, I now wanted to know what was going on up on this roof.

"What are these machines, Axel, and what do they do?"

He explained they were ak aks, and that they were big guns trying to prevent the enemy airplanes from raining bombs on our town. That made me happy, and I felt quite safe being with my beautiful soldiers who protected our town, my family and me. I was convinced that nothing bad could happen to us a long as these brave soldiers sat on the roof of the Kaufhof behind their anti-aircraft guns shooting enemy planes down before they could hurt us.

After my visit with the soldiers and after promising to come back for another visit, I ran home to tell everyone about "my" soldiers on the roof of the Kaufhof. I told them about Axel and how much I liked him and how kind all the soldiers had been to me.

Both my mother and grandparents scolded me for climbing up on the roof of the Kaufhof, and that I no right to do that. I did not understand their anger at all. The soldiers had been so wonderful to me, what was wrong with that? And my father was a soldier, and he would not have minded his daughter to become friends with other soldiers, so I reasoned.

But then my grandmother said: "Inge, I'll go over there and apologize. Those soldiers have been there a long while now, they have a job to do, that little stinker should not have bothered the men."

I was totally insulted! The soldiers liked me, and I did not bother them. They would have told me. So, my grandmother insisted I come along, and we went to the third floor for the second time that day.

The men were astonished to see my grandmother, but when they saw me behind her, they relaxed. They said there was no need to apologize and they enjoyed having me. Axel said all of them had families of their own, and to spend time with a little girl was a welcome interruption. I think they missed their own children, and spending a little time with me was a way to connect with life as it once had been.

My grandmother was satisfied after having been assured by my soldiers that I was not a nuisance, and from then on, I would visit the soldiers until the day when it was no longer possible. My grandmother often sent cookies along for the men.

I liked all the soldiers, but Axel was my favorite. Every time I visited, my place on his lap was secure. From my perch, I searched the sky for approaching planes. I was happy though that we never encountered any enemy airplanes when I was among the soldiers.

With times becoming more and more perilous, my mother and grandparents decided it was time for me to say goodbye to my new-found friends. The reasoning was that these soldiers were on that roof to prevent enemy planes from dropping their deadly ordinance, and they did not need these interruptions from a curious little girl. Also, even though enemy sorties were flown at night in the early years of the war, the reasoning was that it was not impossible for planes to attack us during the day. And so my visits were aborted with a lot of tears and tantrums on my part. The last time with the soldiers was accompanied by hugs and kisses and good wishes for my soldiers. I never saw any of them again.

Many enemy sorties had flown over Solingen and in 1943 numerous of those raids were at night. But with the British and the Americans joining forces, a formidable Air Force was formed which was able with relative accuracy to destroy almost any building they chose. A lot of these raids were directed at Flak units all over Germany. I don't know what happened to the Flak defenders on top of the Kaufhof, but I will never forget them.

Chapter 29

By the fall of 1944, we had run to the bunker several times, and by the end of the war Solingen had been bombed over 90 times. I remember very few of them. One memory I have of those terrible days is the constant feeling of uncertainty, the angst of the adults around me and my continual yearning for my dad's return.

The Solingen population was well aware of the escalation of air raids and bombardments on Cologne, Duesseldorf, Wuppertal and the Ruhr Valley, all areas and cities in our extended neighborhood. But so far Solingen was relatively unharmed. This was about to change.

Saturday, November fourth, 1944, 1:55 pm. It was a beautiful fall day. The sun was shining and people were enjoying their midday meal.

My family and I were sitting around the kitchen table finishing our dinner, which was always served during the middle of the day. My grandparents were talking about the bombing of Remscheid in the summer of 1943. This raid was especially painful for my grandmother, Remscheid was her hometown. Thankfully she did not have any relatives in Remscheid.

Then the sirens sounded again alerting us to approaching enemy airplanes. I remember no one being too excited about that hated sound, the Solingers had become almost lethargic, we had heard the sirens so many times.

Solingen had been attacked by smaller bombing formations, but most of them had been blasted by various Flak battalions and damage was averted.

But since the conversation had just been about the destruction of Remscheid, my grandmother insisted that we go to the shelter. We went on our way, more or less speedily, and were almost not able to reach the bunker. Only a short time after the sirens had raised their warning, we heard the bombers approaching from the distance. Up to this point I had never seen the planes, and the idea of seeing the

116

enemy planes was the scariest thing I could imagine. I knew the bombers came to hurt us, so I ran as fast as I could up the stairs into the bunker, and entered safety even before my mother and grandmother. I noticed other people came running from all directions and begged for the door to stay open. My grandfather, against his better judgment, kept the doors open until the last person had made it in.

The planes were now over us, and since the doors were still slightly open, I saw them for a split second. I remember feeling so scared, I automatically stepped deeper inside the bunker and safety I hoped. The doors shut with its usual squeaking noise which I had heard before, my mother dragged me even deeper into the shelter and all of us stood, listening, breathing heavily and frightened. Some of the women and some children were crying, men were cursing the horrible Tommies, which by that time probably had become Amis, since a lot of the sorties were flown by Americans. There was confusion, everyone hoped that Solingen would be spared, even though there had been raids before. So here we were, and we were afraid.

I do not know how long the bombardment lasted, it seemed endless, but eventually the doors were opened and we exited the shelter. The first emotion was – we were happy to see none of our immediate neighborhood had been destroyed. Then we smelled it, the smoke, we saw the red sky not too far in the distance, and we knew Solingen had been hit, but on that day not in my immediate neighborhood.

My family and I made our way back the short way up the hill and to our house. It had withstood the attack. Some of the upstairs windows were shattered, but the large store front window had withstood the battle. We entered the hallway leading to the living quarters.

I do not recall what was said, if anything at all. I think everyone was dealing with the terror of that event in his own way. Even I had not much to say. We went into the kitchen and sat around the table which still had the remnants of our midday meal on it. My mother and her sister cleared off the table, my grandmother put the kettle on the stove. Thank goodness, it worked. She then made a cup of hot chocolate for me and tea for the adults.

After a while, sipping our brews, the conversation began. Quietly at first, then more animated.

"What happened," was the first thing my mother said, "why Solingen?"

"Inge, you can't be that naive. There are factories in Solingen whose only job it is to manufacture war materials, and I think those places were hit today. I could see the south part of Solingen in flames when we came out of the bunker. Thankfully, we are a bit further north, but who knows when it will hit us?"

"Well, there are no factories in the center of town, so if they destroyed those places, why would they come back here? What can they gain from a bunch of small businesses that have not been open for quite some time," my mother asked.

"Let it be, child," my grandmother replied. "Let's just hope that this damned war comes to an end soon."

I think I was too scared about what we just had witnessed to object to my grandmother's language. I had never heard her curse before.

My grandfather left the kitchen and opened the front door, stepped outside and looked around. I had followed him to the front door, but did not dare to set a foot outside. I watched him, and I realized that he was distraught by what he saw. He just stood there and shook his head as if he just could not believe his eyes.

I stuck my head a bit further out of the door and saw what had him so upset. The entire sky in the distance was in flames, a frightful sight. My beloved Solingen had been severely wounded. I walked back into the kitchen, sat next to my grandmother on the sofa and cried.

The window panes were not repaired that day, my grandfather closed the shutters to keep as much of the cold out as possible. Eventually my mother took me upstairs to bed, and I asked her to stay with me until I fell asleep.

"Are we safe tonight, Mutti," I asked, "or will we have to get up again to run to the bunker?"

She assured me that we would be safe that night, she said the Tommies had used up all their bombs for the day, and they had to fly far away over an ocean to get more. I was appeased, but I did ask her to play my favorite song on the piano in the living room and sing "Mamatschi". She did, but her voice sounded different tonight. I think she was sad.

Chapter 30

The following day my grandparents sat on the sofa in our upstairs living room, while my aunt Christl and I occupied two easy chairs. My mother was away visiting friends somewhere in another part of Solingen. The adults discussed the events from the previous day, even I was allowed to vent my anger at these awful "Tommies" who caused us so much grief.

The radio was on, but the volume was turned down low. The cold November air was streaming through the broken windows After discussing yesterday's air raid for some time, my grandfather changed the subject.

"How is your training going, Christl," he asked.

My aunt, who was in the third year of her apprenticeship with another master beautician in Merscheid, a suburb of Solingen, rolled her eyes as if to say you know very well how it is going. I know you keep close watch over my progress. But with the courtesy afforded a parent she did not dare to be flippant.

"It seems endless, but I will be done in a few months. I wish you would allow me to finish with you. You're a master barber, and your beauticians can teach me the same things I am learning in Merscheid. I am done with my coloring and permanent waves already. I should not have to stay the whole three years over there when I could finish with you," she complained.

It was useless to talk to him about that topic, and Christl knew only too well what his reaction would be. It followed immediately.

"If you want to become a master of your craft, you will finish your apprenticeship where you are. There is no shortcut, and one does not interrupt one's apprenticeship. Then you will absolve five years of journeyman, which you can do here, then you can apply to make your master's. That is how it is done, and that is what you will do."

That was the end of the conversation as far as my grandfather was concerned. I thought he was a little harsh with my aunt, not his usual reserved self. But after the horrible events of the previous day, he was on edge and was not going to have his daughter tell him how things were done in the beauty business.

Christl stubbornly made one more attempt at convincing her father otherwise.

"Inge helps you and she did not have to go through all this stuff," she pouted with her arms crossed in defiance.

She was about to have a stern lesson in paternal child rearing when something on the radio interrupted their discourse. The announcer alerted us to enemy airplanes in the area. My grandfather looked out of the window noticing people running from their homes toward the bomb shelter. It was a little after the noon hour, and the family was just about to have their midday meal in the kitchen downstairs. That was forgotten, and we started to make our way to the bunker.

Chapter 31

There were no sirens this time, the grid had been destroyed the previous day. Nevertheless, better safe than sorry, we ran to the bunker.

And this time we did not dawdle. My grandfather ran ahead of us to the bunker to open the iron doors. My grandmother grabbed her bag which was sitting by the front door. My aunt Christl and I followed speedily. I think we all thought the radio must have it wrong, since we were bombed the previous day. The enemy surely would not return another day, we were not that important a target. We were wrong.

Even before we reached the shelter we heard the planes in the distance. No one knew what they would bring and where they would unload their deadly cargo. We all hoped they would pass us by once again.

When we reached the bunker a few minutes later, we saw my grandfather standing by the now open iron doors, and we heard him saying, "are they sleeping up there?" I did not know where "up there" was, it probably had something to do with the sirens that had not alerted us of impending danger.

People were now streaming in from all directions. Men and women running, small children were being carried by the adults, older children were being urged to hurry and keep up.

I was standing close to my grandfather, so I could see a lot of people coming to the bunker from all around us. My grandfather called to them to hurry. When everyone was finally inside, my grandfather closed the iron doors. The doors now had to stay closed, because as my grandfather explained to me some time ago, fire would erupt when bombs hit their targets, the wind would fan the flames, which then would waft inside the bunker, and everyone in the bunker was in danger of being burned.

I remember thinking how much I hoped that everyone had reached the safety of the shelter before the doors had to be shut. Outside noises were muffled at first, but then we heard the terrible sounds of explosions. One bomb after another hit the bunker. We later found out twenty-four bombs hit our bunker that awful November day.

My grandmother and I sat on the bench in the small room to the left of the entrance. The little room had been assigned to the bunker warden and provided privacy. Christl had gone to the subterranean room, and my grandfather stood guard at the door. I was more than happy not to have to sit on the spiral concrete stairs and watch frightened people.

My grandmother held me close to her for a while, telling me over and over that it would soon stop. I think she was trying to convince herself almost more than me. Every new bomb hitting the shelter made me jump. I remember starting to cry, even my grandmother's softly spoken words could not eliminate the fear I felt in this small room, cut off from the outside and everything that was dear to me.

Finally, my grandmother placed a blanket on the small bench and asked me to be good and lie down on the bench. She told me she would be right back, she just had to speak to my grandfather. I lay still for a while, listening to what was going on outside, and wondering if we would be safe once again. When another bomb hit I got off the bench and out of the door to find my family.

As I left the room, I had to squeeze by people who sat closely huddled together on the stairs. I looked around and saw my grandfather by the front door, my grandmother was not with him. I yelled at him, "where is Ommi?"

He answered, but I could not hear his voice in all the din. People were talking to one another, children were crying, bombs were hitting the shelter in intervals making their own terrible noise. I shook my head at my grandfather indicating that I could not hear him, he pointed toward the top of the shelter, I thought she must have searched for someone up there.

So, I climbed all the way to the top of the shelter, where the stairs became narrower with every step I took. The moment I reached the highest point another bomb hit, and I noticed that the top was swaying just as my grandfather had said it would. Alarmed I ran downstairs as fast I could get to him, which was no small feat squeezing myself by all the frightened people who occupied the stairs.

"Oppi, Oppi," I yelled, "the bunker is breaking."

My grandfather took me aside and asked me to not make so much noise. He reminded me that people were frightened enough without his grandchild making such a fuss. He also reminded me that the bunker had to sway, or it would crumble. He said it had something to do with physics. Naturally, I did not understand what physics were, but if he said so, it must be right.

Chapter 32

Finally, my grandmother returned and guided me to the little subterranean room, the caretakers room. It was not any better down here. Frightened people were standing around the oxygen bottles, eyes as big as saucers, and shaking with every new bomb that hit our shelter. We could hear every detonation, and I remember thinking, if the Tommies don't stop soon, they will break the bunker.

I did not like it down here at all. I asked my grandmother if I could go back up to the little room and the cot. She said no she felt safer having me with her down here. So, we sat on the bench, my grandmother, my aunt and I. The fear was palpable and I remember it had an odor. So many frightened people. Even though everyone was trying to keep calm, their faces betrayed them. I remember the hissing sound the oxygen bottles made and people trying get more air to their lungs. With every new bomb that found its target, scared eyes looked upward as if to make sure the ceiling was still in one piece.

All of a sudden there was a disturbance upstairs. Voices were heard, "make way, make way." Then I saw what was happening. Four men were carrying a stretcher on which a woman lay. They placed the stretcher in front of our bench, the horror that met my eyes has stayed with me all of my life.

The woman had severe injuries to her abdomen (later I was told she was hit by a shrapnel). She was wearing a pink corset with stays and ribbons, and I noticed that some of her intestines were oozing through the ribbons and the stays. Her hands were bloody and flailing.

At some point her hands touched my legs. Being six years old and horrified by what I saw, I pulled my legs as far under the bench as I could. I did not want to be touched by her bloody hands. At that precise moment, she looked up at me and with the sweetest smile on her face she said, "yes, child, I know." And with that she closed her eyes and died.

Looking back at that terrible day, I wish I would have been kinder and would have taken her hand. The only justification I have – I was a child and I was terrified.

They finally covered the poor woman with something, I think it was someone's coat.

My grandmother had been trying to cover my eyes, but I saw, and it was the most terrifying thing I had ever witnessed.

The bunker upstairs was filled to capacity, there just was no room to place the stretcher, so they brought this poor, unfortunate women downstairs. I wish they had not done that.

For weeks after this terrible event I had dreams of a burnt-out forest, with nothing but charred trees, and in that desolate place, devoid of anything pleasant, I saw a woman walking with long gray hair and a flowing white robe – she was singing. I don't know what this recurring dream meant, I just wondered why would anyone in their right mind sing surrounded by charred trees.

The dream stopped after some months, but it did bother me. I never told my family about the dream. Maybe I should have, but in those terrible days I had learned to keep a lot to myself.

We sat on the bench for some while yet, the stretcher with the dead woman in front of my feet. I tried not to look at it, but I knew it was there. I started crying uncontrollably, my grandmother held me close telling me repeatedly, "it will all be over soon."

I don't know how long we stayed in that small room. When we heard the the iron doors finally opened, I tore myself from my grandmother's hands and ran upstairs as fast as I could squeeze myself by the adults who were trying to get out of the bunker as well. All I could think of was to get away from the horror I had seen downstairs.

Chapter 33

Upon exiting the bunker, we were faced with an inferno. There were fires everywhere, not one structure in the neighborhood unharmed. Nothing but rubble and ashes. For a moment, we stood in the doorway, almost pushed over by people trying to get out. We did not know what to do or where to go. We had no home to which to run.

My grandmother took my hand and led me down the stairs to a place in front of the bunker where the fires had not reached. We were not able to move in any direction. The fires were too close, and it was dangerous to leave the area immediately around the bunker. We huddled on the ground together for hours, too dazed to even be aware of people around us, staring at the total destruction we saw before us. Neither one of us spoke.

Suddenly my grandfather pointed in a vague direction to our left and said with a deep sigh,

"I think our home was up there somewhere."

There was no longer a point of reference, no way to tell where our beautiful house once stood. In one night, our entire neighborhood was destroyed.

How could this be? Solingen had just been bombed the previous day. Why again?

My grandmother was crying silently when my grandfather put his arms around her shoulders and said,

"Don't cry, Jenny, at least we are all together."

His life's work lay in ruins before our eyes, and he was still able to comfort his wife and family.

My mother was not with us, and I was worried. While writing this book at one time I asked my husband if he thought it was odd that I did not remember the emotions I felt on that night. I recall all that was going on around me on the singed grass, but my emotions to this day are a foggy. I cried a lot during earlier air raids, when my father left us when I had to get up from a deep sleep once more to run to the shelter, but not that night.

That poor woman who died in front of my feet had touched me so deeply, I think my emotions after that event were drained to the point of not feeling much of anything. I remember thinking very rationally for a six-year-old, 'where will we live now, we must find a house.'

No one really dared to venture further out for fear that the fires all around us would consume us also. Flames and phosphorus puddles made it almost impossible to step away from the immediate area around the bunker. The grass that once was all around the bunker was singed.

A lot of people were coughing, as was I, the smoke irritated our lungs and the smell of burning wood was everywhere. My grandmother placed a damp handkerchief on my mouth and nose. It did not help. I still remember the smell of that night.

Silent conversation was all around us, I don't think my family spoke much. My grandmother had stopped her heartbreaking sobs, her shoulders stopped shaking as she took interest in her surrounding and her family. She looked at my aunt Christl whose face resembled a Chimney sweep covered with soot and ashes, and she actually smiled. I believe we all had that same look, but nobody cared.

It had gotten dark, we were hungry and thirsty. My grandmother looked for her valise she had brought with her from the house. She had placed it next to her on the ground. The valise was gone. Even with terrible things happening to everyone, someone had stolen her cherished bag. It had stood by our front door for months, she told me it held a dress and slippers for me, as well as her beloved silverware, cutlery made in Solingen, of course, and some dried items like crackers and such. Well, it too was gone now, so we really only owned the clothes we were wearing.

I looked at my grandmother and saw small pieces of ash carried by the wind landing on her hair, and I fought the urge to laugh. My sweet grandmother, the most fastidious woman I knew, was covered with small pieces of debris, and she did not seem to care. I remember I brushed the ashes off her head, she smiled at me, and said, "it doesn't matter, child." We both knew the important thing - we were alive.

I was hot on that cold November day. The fires all around generated an immense heat.

I saw neighbors sitting on the ground, hollow-eyed, without aim or purpose. One lady stood up, mumbling, "I have to leave, I have to find my family." Others just nodded, but no one moved. These were the Germans of the glorious Third Reich, defeated, beaten down and without resolve. I don't know how many of our fellow citizens had belonged to the National Socialistic Party of Hitler and his henchmen, neither did I know what any of that meant anyway, but they were not the super race that Hitler tried to make them believe they were. They were as pitiful a group of humans as I had ever seen.

It was difficult to see all the destruction all around us, and it was almost unbearable to see the dead bodies strewn around the bunker. Thankfully someone had covered their faces, and my grandfather tried his best to shield me from that horror. But how does one erase such a sight.

The dust and the ashes made it difficult to breathe, and our throats were hurting. There was no water. I was hungry and thirsty, more thirsty than hungry actually. I don't remember when we finally, a day later, we saw help arriving in the form of a Red Cross truck with metal barrels full of barley soup, as well as cheese sandwiches and cool, fresh water for our parched throats.

Everyone marched in perfect order to the truck. No one was pushing or trying to get to the food ahead of anyone else. People were much too discouraged and weary. There was no need for pushing anyway, because there was enough food for the throng of about a hundred or so people. Some folks had already left the area in spite of the bunker personnel telling them it was too dangerous to leave.

And so, the rest of us received a bowl of soup and a sandwich. It was the most delicious meal I had ever tasted. Although, there were one or two tiny pebbles in the soup. Most of all we all appreciated the water. And the fact that we were not forgotten, even in this hell.

After a while when the fires burnt out and we could see clearly, we were finally able to walk around a bit further. We climbed the small hill that led to the place where our house once stood. With all the horrible things I had seen and heard up to now, the complete destruction of my grandparents' beautiful house was more than I could take. I remember crying so hard, my grandmother tried to stifle my sobbing by placing her hand softly over my mouth. She rocked me back and forth to quiet me, and after a while I sat down on a mound of rubble.

I did not think that anything could ever be normal again. My beloved hometown was destroyed, our beautiful home was gone, my father was away fighting a war which had finally reached us at home in the most terrifying way possible.

All around us were the ruins of once grand Patrician homes staring back at us accusingly as if to ask why did you let this happen?

For the next few days we remained in the bunker together with other families who had lost their homes. Some people left to find shelter with families in other parts of Solingen that had not been bombed as heavily as the town center.

My grandparents decided to stay in the bunker until living quarters could be found. I don't remember how long we were there, but I do recall that I was never going to the downstairs room again. My grandmother allowed me to sleep on the cot upstairs next to the entrance door at night, while she sat on a chair next to the cot. She understood my refusal to enter that room again where I had seen the most horrible sight of my young life.

Some days later my mother had made her way to the bunker, I don't know how she managed to make her way through Solingen, but she did. She had been visiting friends on the outskirts of Solingen before the bombing. I was so happy to see my mother, I told her of all the awful things I had seen, that I wanted my father, and that I thought war the most awful thing that could happen to people, until she finally stopped me. She hugged me tightly and told me how sorry she was that I had to witness all those horrendous things, then she softly sang my favorite song to me with her voice breaking.

In the following days, I had a new worry enter my restless mind. How would my father find us when he came home from the war? We did not have a house anymore. There was no need to worry, but I did not know this at that time.

My mother and grandmother were content with staying in the bunker until we could find if not a house, at least an apartment.

I do not recall what we ate or anything else about our daily lives. I had found my old friend, Gabi, again. Her family, whose house was on our street as well and was totally destroyed, had found housing with family in another part of our town. However, they knew of our plight and came to visit and Gabi came with them. I was very happy to see my old friend had made it out alive as well. They were in another bunker on that awful day.

In the days following the bombardments on Solingen, the fires were gradually brought under control or burned themselves out. The dust and ashes were gone, and we could now clearly see the destruction. Solingen had died.

My grandfather left every day and walked all over town to find living quarters for us. It was an impossible task.

I have often wondered how my courageous family held out under all that stress. No one was angry, no one bickered, even Christl did not pinch my nose as for some reason she had always liked to do. We walked through the hours and days almost aimlessly, lost in a world of nefariousness.

131

I repeated one thought I had over and over to the adults in my family, if my father would have been here our house would not have been destroyed. I was sure of it. Little girls think their fathers are more than human.

Chapter 34

In the following weeks, we had to adjust to our changed circumstances. From somewhere blankets, pillows, clothing, food and water, as well as some of the most necessary toiletries appeared daily. I don't know who sent all these things, but whoever these angels were, I hope they were richly rewarded.

I recall we took short walks through the rubble that had once been my beloved hometown. We did not dare to venture too far from the protection of the bunker. Only my grandfather still would walk all over town to find living quarters.

What we saw during those excursions was truly heartbreaking. Gone was my cherished department store, only a burned-out shell remained. It had retained some of the outer walls and the ceiling of the first floor. I wondered where my soldier friends had gone and did they make it off the roof in time?

The casino that once stood proudly across from the Kaufhof was an empty shell. Our beautiful Gothic church was severely damaged, most of the stained-glass windows were destroyed, and the steeples had been lost as well. Destruction everywhere one looked in the inner city. When walking a bit toward the north city we actually found some buildings miraculously unharmed, but for the most part the city lay in ruins.

Chapter 35

Soon the debris of brick and mortar, metal beams sticking out of ruins like long, dark fingers became almost a bit trite. I guess it is generally accepted that Germans are an industrious people, so the surviving city fathers did not take long to form an interim government. The leaders of the town asked every citizen to take part in the resurrection of Solingen. We were asked to clean useable bricks, of which there was no shortage. Wherever we found them, we sat and hammered mortar off the bricks. It helped to pass the time, we were in fresh air, a definite improvement from the dank and musty smell of the bunker. We never walked too far from the security of the bunker. There still was a war going on, and even though I could not see any reason for the enemy to return to Solingen, unless they wanted to kill every German in it.

The November air was cold, but we did not complain. We had come through hell, we had lost everything, but were alive. Thinking back on a quote from King Solomon comes to mind "vanity, vanity, all is vanity". Even today, I am not particularly attached to material things, I had learned that they can all be taken away from you at a moment's notice.

There were quite a few more air raids until the war finally ceased in 1945, but they became more sparingly in our area. The first raid in December of 1943 took place when 60-80 planes came from the West to attack Solingen and were stopped by Flak battalions. There were several raids throughout the region without doing a lot of damage until the two main bombardments on November 4 and 5, 1944 which destroyed the town. The steel giants of Solingen had been slain, the inhabitants demoralized.

My family and I lived in the shelter for many months. After a while it almost seemed normal to call a bomb shelter home. Frequently we searched the spot where once had stood my grandparents' home and business in hope to find something useful. There was nothing to be found.

The street itself had been widened considerably by the sheer absence of buildings. We could see far beyond where once had been our neighborhood, and it always gave me a feeling of vast emptiness, so different from the intimate surrounding of our little street.

We walked through the ruins, scraping at dirt and rubble, until one day we found one little kitchen tile. I looked at my grandmother's face and saw a single tear running down her cheek. It made me so sad. This brave woman had to face loss of her cherished home and now was forced to live in a dark and damp bomb shelter, and all of it through no fault of her own. She never belonged to a political party in her life.

I put my hand into hers and dragged her away from the ruins. There was no reason to stay here any longer. We walked back down the hill to the bunker.

All of us had cots, blankets and pillows given to us by kind people who had heard that my family had not been able to find living quarters and still lived in the bunker. Naturally we were not the only ones, so many people had lost their homes on those two early November days, but at least we were not living on the streets.

Chapter 36

While living in the shelter I had developed an obsession for building little structures of used brick (there was no shortage of bricks) and whatever building material I could find. I was not alone. There were four of us, all children who had lost their homes, Rainer, Gitte, Beate and I worked together to make a small shelter.

We stacked the brick to build three walls leaving one side open for access. We found a sheet of corrugated metal in the ruins to serve as our roof. To cover the entrance, we found a burlap sack to shield us from rain and snow.

We sat in this hide out for hours, right in the middle of an ash covered rubble field, talked about the war and what we had experienced, hopefully better times ahead for all of us, but mostly we talked about the hope to see our dads again (none of our fathers ever returned). I was almost sad to leave this little hut that four children had fashioned out of rubble. But soon we were all to move away.

One day, as we were playing in our hut, my mother and grandmother came to visit, and I overheard my mother saying," look at these children – they're playing in the rubble of war."

Chapter 37

I was fighting my way over a mountain of debris to our little hide-out, when I saw two men walking hastily down the street next to the bunker. The men were strangers to me, I had never seen them before. In the vicinity of the shelter we all knew each other, but my mother had alerted me never to talk to strangers during this time of uncertainty. I did not heed her warning and approached the strangers to find out if they were lost. There was nothing but ruins and rubble all around, maybe these men were looking for their home.

"Are you searching for your family, I asked?"

To my great surprise and horror, one of the men addressed me and said, "Mind your own business, little girl. Go home and you better not tell anyone that you have seen us. If you tell, we will come back tonight, kill you and chop you into little pieces. We will stuff you into our bag and toss you in a river."

They had to be really lost, the nearest river was ten miles away. But I was six years old, so naturally, I believed them. Petrified I started to cry, running toward the shelter and was screaming for my mother. The men ran away, I noticed the direction toward which they were running. My mother had heard me scream and came flying out of the shelter.

"What is the matter, are your hurt?"

"They're coming tonight, and they will cut me into little pieces, "I sobbed.

My mother tried to get some coherent information from me, and under sobs I told her what had just transpired. She became very still, called for my grandfather, who happened to be in the bunker that day, and we all sped into the direction I had seen the men run.

By now we were no longer alone. All my yelling and screaming had attracted some of the people around, and everyone helped us to look for the strangers. They were soon found in the bombed-out shell of a former clothing store. When I had identified them, I was sent back to the shelter accompanied by a family friend.

Later I was told the men were apprehended. I was never told who they were or what happened to them. After this frightening event, my mother insisted even more sternly that I was never, ever to talk to strangers.

The next day, I went to our hide-out. My friends were already there, and my adventure from the previous day was told. I was a hero that day. Had I not single-highhandedly brought two scoundrels to justice. At least that's how my friends saw it. I am sure I embellished the narrative.

I have never forgotten those days in the field of ashes and rubble, feeling protected by three brick walls without mortar and a metal roof in the circle of my friends.

Chapter 38

I have often overheard family and friends speaking of their war experience. Questions like how did it come to this, and didn't our leaders promise us a utopian Germany, were asked over and over. I wondered why the adults had believed all the propaganda? Didn't they know when the war came to the "fatherland" that it was over for the Germans?

But even though I referred to the enemy as "Tommies" when I was a child, as an adult I never blamed the allies for the destruction they rained on my beloved hometown. I was resigned as a child and enlightened as an adult. I accepted that Germany was the aggressor and had to be brought to her knees.

I also realized that collateral damage had to occur in order to stop the Nazi war machine. The death of totally guiltless human beings, old men and women, as well as children is never easy to justify. Also, it is not easy to accept that our young men were sent to war to be annihilated on foreign battlefields because a ruthless government wished it. But when I much later learned of the atrocities this same government had committed I knew I was right in condemning Germany and the war it had started.

Not all of our young men were members of the dreaded SS, or in any way connected to the politics of the Nazi regime. Most of them were courageous young men who believed in a reborn Germany after the tragic events of WWI. Toward the end of the war these young men and children, some as young as twelve years old, were thrown into the fray, merely as cannon fodder because a corrupt and evil regime ordered it.

Chapter 39

That year, 1944, we were still living in the bunker when Christmas came around. Christmas 1944 was nothing like the holidays we had celebrated in our home before. My father still had not returned from the battlefield, and we had not had a message from him for a long time. I missed my father so much. My mother and grandmother tried their best to make the holiday festive.

There was a small tree without candles or ornaments, but at least we had a real Christmas tree. There also was a gift for me under our little evergreen tree, a little red riding hood doll my grandmother had fashioned from rags she found somewhere. She had also baked cookies in someone else's oven. We called them consumption cookies, due to their pale color. They were made without eggs or butter, but they tasted like manna from heaven. Finally, a sugary treat, no matter how dry they were. On this Christmas Eve, we sang carols and ate our cookies, and tears were shed by almost everyone. But we were thankful to be alive and somewhat warm in that damp bunker. So many Solingers had been killed this year.

One day in early January of 1945 my grandfather came to the shelter after one of his house hunting excursions and brought us the most welcome news in a long while. He had found an apartment for us in the North part of the town. He had also found a location not far from the apartment where he could open a new barber shop and beauty salon. We were elated, and my grandparents, Christl and I soon left the dark and inhospitable bomb shelter behind and moved a few of our belongings into our new home. My mother refused to leave the safety of the shelter.

The bunker kept us safe, but with all the horrible sights I associated with this place, I was more than happy to leave it behind. Even after the war I have never been back to visit the bomb shelter. It was demolished sometime in the 1950s, at which time I had already moved to Cologne to live with my mother.

The new apartment was far from the luxurious home my grandparents owned. It was on the second floor and extremely small.

There was one bedroom, a living room and a kitchen toward the back of the building. There was no bathroom, just a powder room with a sink and a toilet.

But as small as it was, it was better by far than the bomb shelter. We shared the floor with another family, with three children, one of whom was a girl my own age, a brother and an older sister. The girl later became my best friend and I am in contact with her to this day.

The living room faced toward the front of the five-story building looking down on a very busy street. Under two relatively large windows were built-in bookcases running along the entire wall. My grandfather had found a radio somewhere and we housed it in the bookcase. A radio was a very important commodity in those days, and we were very careful not to let too many people know that we had one. We listened to radio London (I think that' was what it was called), which was strictly forbidden to do for the German populace. But everyone listened to it anyway. I don't think my family was afraid of too much anymore. We came alive out of two bombardments, had lost our home and at this point lived of the kindness of strangers, there was not much the Nazi Regime could do to us. So we thought. We did not know that the war was to go on for months yet.

My mother, in wise anticipation, had not given up our base in the shelter. She told us that as long as the war was still going on, she would not leave the shelter.

Back in the apartment, which my grandfather was able to secure from a beautician who had worked for him some years ago and whose husband owned the large building, my grandmother and I tried to make things as comfortable and homey as we could.

There was a large bed in the bedroom, and a smaller one on one side under a window looking out on a huge Chestnut tree and the Solinger Opera house and Theater. My grandparents occupied the large bed, and I slept in the smaller one. There was also a large wardrobe to hang our clothes, such as they were.

In the living room, there was a sofa, a round table with four chairs and two easy chairs under the windows with a coffee table between them. And lo' and behold, in the corner stood a piano. From where did all this furniture come, I wondered, but I did not delve into their origin too far. We had furniture and an actual home again, far, far better than living in the bunker.

In the kitchen were two cabinets which held some dishes and pots. There was a sink and a country table with chairs, as well as a wood stove, on which my grandmother would cook our meals.

Dear Reader, at this point you probably wonder how did these people clean themselves and take a bath? There was no bathtub in our apartment. Well, we would wash every day in the kitchen under cold water, and once a week my grandparents would bring in a large galvanized metal tub in which they would pour hot water, heated on the coal stove and enough cold water to make the bath comfortable. And all of this was much better than no baths in the shelter.

Thinking about those Spartan accommodations, I am reminded how awful it must have been for my grandparents, and especially my beloved grandmother who loved a beautiful home more than anything in the world. I was a child, with childlike thinking. As long as my family was with me and we had a home again, my world was bearable, and one day when my Dad would return my life was going to be bliss. The horrible events I had to witness in the bunker were not forgotten, but placed in a corner of my brain where I did not want to visit often.

Outside of our living room was a long corridor, probably forty feet long from which the rooms of our neighbors branched off. This living arrangement is not unusual in Germany. The country is approximately the size of Texas, but has to house many millions of Germans. And unless one is independently wealthy and can afford to live in a house, the Germans make their homes in apartment buildings.

Naturally, during the war years with so many homes lost to allied strikes, things became even more claustrophobic.

142

Chapter 40

We were glad to have a place we could call home. We had to adjust to the confined space and the absence of a bathroom, but we made do.

I remember this apartment fondly as a safe haven after a terribly unsettling time. I made new friends quickly with our neighbors, especially the brother and sister, a friendship I value to this day.

The war was not over, but our city had been destroyed and there really was no point for the enemy to return. Everything would have been satisfactory had it not been for my mother. She would come to visit the apartment, but she refused to stay overnight. She said as long as the war was raging, she did not feel safe outside of the bunker.

I believe she was severely traumatized, I think today we would refer to this state of mind as post-traumatic stress syndrome. The constant air raids, her husband away somewhere in a foreign country fighting this infernal war, no food (or very little), and the enemy approaching ever closer into Germany, the annihilation of her hometown on those two terrible November days, all led to her anxiety. For all of these reasons she stayed in the bunker.

My grandparents decided that I should live with them in the apartment in much better conditions. My mother agreed, although she insisted that my grandmother would bring me to the bunker daily. My grandmother said it would only be a little while, and then my mother would "come to her senses"

Even though neither one in my family had belonged to the Nazi party, and I am not aware of anyone behaving in any way that could be seen as offensive, my mother was afraid that the enemy would arrest all of us, simply for being German.

My very intelligent mother felt guilty for something she did not do or cause. Eventually, people would give this condition a name, they called it "collective guilt". Many Germans of that time know the feeling well. I was blissfully unaware of the dark side of the regime and the unspeakable horror they inflicted on an innocent people. During my school years nothing of that was taught. Unbelievable as this seems, I learned about the holocaust when I emigrated to the United States in 1965. I did not believe the things I heard, until I educated myself on the subject, and there is probably not much written about the holocaust I have not read.

However, this book was not written to address the awful deeds that were committed by a murderous group of people and the almost total extinction of an entire people in Europe.

Chapter 41

My grandmother devised a system how to feed the entire family, including my mother in the bunker. She would cook a meal on the coal stove and she and I would take the food to the bunker once a day, about two miles from the apartment. I did not know where the food for these meals originated, but somehow, we always had sustenance. I remember that we did not have meat very often, once a month in the beginning meat appeared on the table. We ate a lot of potatoes in all forms, my favorite were her delicious potato pancakes. I really did not care whether we had meat or fish, as long as we had something to sustain us.

Children adjust rather quickly to changed circumstances, but how awful it must have been for my family to live in very much less luxurious conditions, but I have never heard any of them complain.

So my grandmother and I made our daily trips to the bomb shelter to bring food to my mother. On one such day we had completed our grocery shopping in town (little mom and pop stores had sprung from practically nowhere), we walked back to the apartment and my grandmother started to cook. I was visiting my new friend on the same floor where we lived with the admonition no to stray too far away in case of alarms. They still came frequently, most not meant for us, however.

All of a sudden, we heard the before alarm close by. My grandmother immediately doused the flames on the stove, called for me in the hallway, and off we went running toward the bunker. There had been no time to change into street shoes, I was wearing my house slippers.

It had been decided that my grandfather would lock the salon doors and make his way to the bunker, we would do the same. Recently, again, we had sort of disregarded the alarms, I do not know what made this day different. We ran as fast as we could to try to reach the shelter in time, the sound of the sirens urging us to run ever faster. We did not make it.

We reached the Kaufhof, my once favorite department store, now a skeleton with only the roof and the outside walls standing. We could hear the bombers right above us. My grandmother pulled me into the shell of the Kaufhof, and we instantly fell to the floor, pressing our bodies flat to the concrete slab. There were other people lying next to us, frightened, shaking and watching the bombers flying above us awaiting the destruction that was sure to follow. The deafening noise of exploding implements of war was all around us. Death was raining down in the form of incendiaries and bombs crashing, detonating as soon as they hit their target. I heard screaming from the people next to us. I looked up to see where the screams originated. As far as I could tell no one was hurt, but the look in their eyes told the story. Complete panic set in, and people were starting to get up and run. My grandmother kept me tightly next to her on the concrete.

Across from the department store stood the ruin of a once elegant casino. I saw two German officers in uniform standing in the damaged doorway of the casino. Their binoculars were trained on the planes above.

I was petrified and I remember thinking "Stop, stop, we haven't done anything to you, stop, stop hurting us." They did not stop, although, the entire raid probably did not last longer than a few minutes.

Fires were all around us, and this time I saw the inferno from the outside, not from the safety of the bunker. I have never experienced anything so frightening in my life. The noise alone was ear-splitting. Phosphorus puddles glowing greenish all around the building. The ground shook every time a bomb hit its target, whining and whistling just before it exploded.

Even after the planes had left our immediate area, my grandmother and I were still on our spot on the concrete. At times, during the raid, my grandmother shielded me with her own body holding her hands over my ears. My grandmother will always be my hero.

The fires and phosphorus were encroaching on our position. The bombers had delivered their ordinance and had left our air space. But now we had a new problem, how could we get to the bunker without stepping into the fiery puddles all around us. The bunker was now about a hundred yards away from us. My grandmother pulled me up and started to exit the building when we heard loud voices from across the street.

"Hin legen, hin legen!" (lie down, lie down) the order came from the officers in the casino ruin. Well, a lot of times, in Germany, when an officer gives you an order, whether one is in the military or not, one obeys. Not this time!

My grandmother was not to be deterred or ordered about by military personnel. She had seen so much pain and agony during the past year, she had had enough. And with a strong voice she looked at me and said, "Child, can you run with Ommi?" I only nodded and we started running toward the bunker with its thick concrete walls and the safety behind them.

It was treacherous to run under these conditions. We tried to avoid stepping into the greenish glowing hot phosphorus, when one of my slippers caught fire. I screamed pointing at my foot and the burning slipper. My grandmother tore my slippers of my foot, caught me up with one arm, and carried me like a sack of potatoes, running. She was breathing deeply, but she kept running.

We made it to the bunker, the doors were closed as usual. My grandmother knew which door was guarded by my grandfather, she put me down and we both raced up the stairs to the iron door. We screamed and yelled and then – we had our miracle. The doors opened, we stumbled inside, and my grandmother collapsed, unconscious. My grandfather caught her and brought her to the cot in the little room to the left of the door. Seeing my grandmother looking more dead than alive was more frightening to me than the entire terror filled time in the Kaufhof.

They tried to take me away from her. I was not to be budged, I clung to the sleeve of her coat yelling at the top of my lungs, "Ommi, Ommi, please don't die, please don't die."

She opened her eyes, smiled at me and said," I'll be fine, child, don't make so much noise." My grandmother recovered, however, her heart was never the same.

Once I was assured that she would be well, I sat next to her on a chair, and did not leave her side. After a while they opened the doors once again, and again we walked out to devastation. Much the same as we had seen before, there were the fires, and ashes, but thankfully, we did not see anyone hurt.

Chapter 42

The aftermath of this raid on Solingen stayed with me for quite a while. My mother told me often that I became withdrawn, sullen and uncommunicative. Today one would take a child to a counselor which might have helped, but during this time of war that was not an option. Fears and terrors were with us until the war's end in May of 1945. My family tried to console me, telling me that the war was finally over. I did not believe them. Why was my dad not home if the war was over?

Germany capitulated and it was time for healing and rebuilding. As for me – I learned to live with nightmares and night terrors for a long time.

My mother finally gave up her space in the bunker and came to live with us in the apartment. She soon realized that no former enemy even had the most remote interest in arresting her. We were all excited to have her with us, especially since we did not have to go to the shelter any longer.

Our living space became a bit more cramped, the two sisters shared the sofa to sleep on at night. It was a very large sofa, almost like a daybed, so it was not too uncomfortable for my mother and Christl.

One day Christl met a British soldier, Bill. Soon the two were inseparable. My grandparents invited some of Bill's fellow soldiers, all military police, to a get-together. There were about ten or twelve soldiers all cramped into our small apartment. This event was an attempt at healing wounds between former adversaries. It was surprising to listen to some of the conversations in broken German, and it became quite clear that these British soldiers were amazed to learn that not all Germans were Nazis.

Christl and Bill soon married and moved to England. My mother opened a clothing store in Cologne. She rented a war-damaged house with the stipulation that she would repair the damage. The landlord was happy to have her since an empty house attracted unsavory elements. He wanted his property looked after, and my mother was happy to comply. She enjoyed being in business.

I continued to live with my grandparents which was the best situation for all concerned. I attended the same Elementary School and later High School. My mother visited us most weekends, and I was always elated to see her.

Sometime after the end of the war, I was sent to the country. My grandmother had relatives in Westphalia who lived in a rural area. I was not too keen on leaving her, but after I was told it was for my health, and I would be home again soon, I looked forward to my visit in a place that had been untouched by the war. My grandparents wanted me in a different setting than war-torn Solingen.

I had the best time of my young life on that farm. I learned to ride bareback on a beautiful, gentle horse, I climbed onto a walnut tree and picked walnuts, ate real ham sandwiches and slept in a bed with white as snow linens. The people treated me as one of their own, and when the time came for me to go home, I was sad, but looking forward to seeing my family again. The first thing I asked my grandmother was, "could we go live on that farm forever?"

To this day I have wanted to live on a farm with horses, goats, chickens, dogs and cats. So far, my husband and I have only accomplished to live in a small town here in Pennsylvania with three German Shepherds, naturally, and a calico cat, the dogs were given to us by dear friends.

Chapter 43

Back in Solingen and missing the farm, the nice people and the animals, it was a different story. No more ham, or fresh eggs and cakes that were always baking in the farm oven. Now back at home it fell to me to help out. At times, I was drafted to provide greens for my family. Not store bought, but handpicked in the fields around Solingen. My grandmother sent me to pick nettles. My harvest was always bountiful, since nettles grew in abundance. Not too many people want to touch nettles. If one did not wear gloves, one would pay the price in the form of blistered skin, an unpleasant experience. My grandmother knew this, of course, and she had supplied a pair of gloves for me the gather the greens, which she would then turn into something resembling spinach. Delicious actually. Well, I did not want to wear these bothersome gloves, and I had to bear the consequences. I guess, one learns by doing.

The nettle dish was usually accompanied by some kind of potato dish. Potatoes were sometimes supplied by me also. There were railway tracks a few streets down from our apartment. A number of us neighborhood children would jump the freight trains rumbling slowly along the tracks, we could always see the one carrying potatoes. We were well aware that what we were doing could be considered stealing, but we had not much to eat and we were always hungry. So, we stilled our consciences by convincing ourselves that no one would miss a few potatoes we hid in our coat pockets or sometimes a piece of coal or two going AWOL. The trains moved slowly, so the danger was not great of hurting ourselves.

When taking my little treasures to my grandmother, I committed another sin. I told her I found the potatoes. I doubt, she believed me, but she smiled, and went into a narrative of why we should never take anything which did not belong to us. I listened, but was not convinced that she was angry with me. She cooked the potatoes. War makes us do a lot of things of which we later are not too proud.

Chapter 44

Toward the end of 1945 we started to feel safer in our town. I finally believed the war was over when military trucks, American and British, rolled through Solingen.

We were now securely housed in our apartment, and as time went on we began to visit friends and relatives who had survived the war and whose homes had escaped bombardment. We were all trying to forget the horrors of war, and even though our lives were far from normal any longer, it was important to try to live as though they were. Occasionally we even laughed again.

We were given the equivalent of $10.00 per person in the household to start life over, there were five of us so $50.00 is what we received from the government. If my grandfather had not opened his business again, I do not see how my grandparents would have managed. Gradually ladies visited the salon to have their hair done, and men had their hair cut, some even allowed themselves to be shaved. Like old times, I thought, but also so very different.

My mother, who was by this time quite busy with her own venture in Cologne, nevertheless came to help out once in a while, until my grandfather could hire more personnel in the salon.

I was always happy to see my mother, but it was better to stay where my schools and my friends were, especially my new-found friends. At that time, I was also obsessed with waiting for my father's return, and how could he find me in Cologne, I reasoned. So, I had to stay in Solingen.

The picture of my beloved Solingen had changed drastically. Where once had stood beautiful Patrician homes, now stood wooden buildings, especially in the business sector of town. It happened very quickly, and before long we were able to purchase some items needed for daily living. The small stores were sparsely stocked, however. We were issued ration cards, and luxuries such as butter, eggs, sugar and milk were rationed, and one of my grandmother's favorite drinks, coffee, was not to be found until much later. Times were difficult for the Germans who were fortunate to escape the war unscathed, few complaints, however, were heard.

Germany had been divided into four sectors. The French held part of the West, the British were in charge of the Rhineland and surrounding areas. The Russians took East Germany including part of Berlin, and the Americans took the southern region of the country, which included the most picturesque areas of the land. They were positioned in the Alpine region including Bavaria. There were some Canadian troops in the Northern part of Germany.

Shortly after war's end, and before my mother had moved to Cologne, she would travel to that northern part and bartered with the Canadian soldiers. She would bring cutlery and silverware to the soldiers, which she had secured from some of our friends who tried to help.

Sometimes she would receive silk hose from the soldiers and cigarettes. She would take these items to the farmers in Oldenburg, a city in the richest farmland in the nation, she would barter her treasures for butter, oil, eggs and other food items one could not find in the cities yet.

Occasionally, I was allowed to accompany her on her barter trips. We would take the trains, which had started to roll again soon after the war ended, and we would visit some of the farms.

We ate strawberries and blueberries, and my mother devised a delicious concoction consisting of raw egg yolk beaten with sugar until it was smooth as silk. The egg whites were also beaten to white mountains of deliciousness and folded into the egg yolk mixture. My mother called it "sugar eggs", and I loved it. I believe she knew this protein rich food would nourish our depleted bodies.

Today we shy away from eating raw eggs, but then it was not unusual to eat many things raw. My father loved steak tartar. I tried it later in life, and I found it very tasty. Those occasional trips to that wonderful area with my mother were special times which I have never forgotten.

Back in Solingen, the citizens had a curfew in the early days after the war. The British imposed strict rules for the citizenry. The victors treated us with civility, but it was obvious no love was lost between our two nations.

Chapter 45

One day, in the summer of 1946, during school vacation, I sat on the steps outside in front of my grandfather's salon. I had taken to this activity for a few weeks, looking up and down the street, waiting for I do not know what. I guess, I was hoping to see my father come down the street.

As I looked to my right, I saw the mailman. He waived at me from the distance, as he had done many days before. This day was different, he waived a piece of mail. My heart began to beat wildly, I just knew he had mail from my father. I ran to meet him, and with a smile he handed me a postcard.

"Maybe this is from your dad, "he said, "even though I cannot read the language. It has your grandfather's old address."

I thanked him and ran back to the salon. My grandmother was there and I yelled, "Ommi, Ommi, Vati wrote a postcard."

I handed her the mail, she took it, tried to read it and looked perplexed. She said," this is not from your dad, it is written in Polish, I believe."

My heart sank. But I told myself it was a postcard from my father, it had to be, there had to be a reason why he wrote in Polish. My grandfather had an acquaintance who spoke Polish fluently, he contacted him the same day. The man came and interpreted the writings on the card. It said the writer would soon be home, he was in desperate need of clothing and shoes, and he gave us his shoe size. It was signed "Lumpi", which reminded my mother of an endearing name she called my father sometimes. This strangely worded document was treated with utmost care.

I was the happiest child. I continued every day that summer to sit on the steps for hours, waiting and waiting and waiting. It was not to be.

We learned only years later that one of my grandfather's former barbers had written the card. Why to us, and why at that time we really never knew. The mystery was solved again much later when my grandfather met this barber's brother. We learned that the barber hat been in a Russian prisoner of war camp, was released, returned home and died soon after that. He had never recovered from his days as prisoner of war.

Things gradually normalized with time. Germany changed its currency from Reichs Mark to Deutsche Mark, and the change allowed us to gain more distance from the awful war years. It was a new beginning for all Germans. Gone were the days when we paid two million Reich Marks for a ride at the fair or seven million Marks to purchase a loaf of bread. Real butter and coffee still took their time to appear on store shelves. Years later I remember my grandmother calling me into the kitchen, where she had brewed her first pot of "real coffee". She also presented me with a slice of delectable sourdough rye bread which all Germans love so much. The bread was topped with "real butter". We both feasted that day. How happy she looked even in her small kitchen!

Chapter 46

Life went on, and in time with new leadership at the helm, Germany rose from the ashes and became a prosperous nation again. I guess the proverbial industrious spirit of the Germans would not lie idle for long.

All I have written in this narrative came from stories that had been related to me by family members or from things that I recalled myself.

Much later I learned from acquaintances that my family had scarcely escaped being sent to camps themselves. My grandparents had refused to heed the regime's order not to do business with Jews. My grandfather continued to cut hair for his Jewish friends, albeit in a different locale. His military patrons, including some officers who probably had been home on furlough, were served in the salon, while some of his Jewish friends waited in the back in the kitchen to have their hair cut. I can only imagine how frightened my grandparents must have been. Had the soldiers known of my grandfather's activity, we would have been in grave trouble.

As for my father's destiny – my father's fate did not become known to me until many years later.

In 1963, I married an American soldier while he was stationed in Germany. Our son was born a year later and soon I moved to America with my husband and son. We settled in Tallahassee, Florida, my husband's home state. The marriage did not last, and in 1977 we divorced. I was employed by a prominent law firm in Tallahassee at that time.

In 1975, I received a letter from my mother who still resided in Cologne, Germany. My mother and I corresponded frequently, but this letter was different and would finally bring closure to an open wound which I had been nursing for a long time.

Beside this letter, the envelope contained my father's Soldbuch, a military official document issued to every soldier upon being drafted. Everything that pertained to my father's life in the German army was logged in this passport from the issuance of clothing, guns, ammunition, as well as entries about his illnesses and injuries contracted during those years, and much more. Included in my mother's letter was my father's driver's license with his photograph removed. My mother was given these documents by the German Red Cross, and I keep them safely stored. I look at these items sometimes and always have the feeling that my beloved father is close to me.

My mother's accompanying letter explained the mystery. Evidently my father had been captured by Yugoslavian partisans somewhere in the Balkans. He was placed into a labor camp in a small town near Zagreb. Somehow, while on day labor away from the camp, he was befriended by a family who spoke a little German. He was due to be transported to Serbia shortly, and since that would probably have meant a death sentence for a German soldier, he asked for asylum from this family, which they granted. My father was hidden in the attic of their house until April 1949, at which time his presence in the house became known to the authorities. He was arrested, along with the woman and her twelve-year-old daughter. Apparently, the husband escaped. Mother and her young daughter absolved a five-year prison sentence for harboring a German soldier. My father was transported to a top security prison in Ljubljana, where he died of "heart failure" on October 30, 1950. He had contracted malaria during a march to the Balkans.

In 1979, I remarried and my husband and I lived in Solingen in 1980 and were visited by the woman and her daughter who had hidden my father in their house. I was told that my father spoke about me often and about his love for his only child.

My father's fate was researched by some of the wonderful attorneys of the law firm who were my employers in the 1970s. Florida politicians and the US State Department also helped, and I am extremely grateful for their assistance. Senator Lawton Chiles, who later became Governor of Florida and Congressman Don Fuqua were leaders in this quest.

Epilogue

After so much war-time drama I would like to tell a little story of Christmas in Germany after the war.

As I mentioned before, Christmas has always been my favorite time of the year. I loved the snow we usually had, and all the wonderful things associated with this holiday.

The war was a memory, painful, but now stored away in my brain and best left alone. I was back in school and tried hard to forget the horrors I had witnessed.

And somehow my dear grandparents were able to restore the mood of that festive season.

Traditionally, the Christmas season began with the first Sunday of Advent. This Sunday was very much anticipated. We had just finished observing all those dreary November days of All Souls, All Saints and the especially drab Totensonntag, all days to commemorate the dear departed. The music on our radio was somber, Beethoven and Wagner were very much in demand.

I drove my grandmother to distraction with my constant questions about the long awaited first Sunday of Advent. That day could never come soon enough.

When it was finally here, usually around the first days of December, all the long and sad days of November with its gray skies and cold, damp temperatures were forgotten. The mood was lifted and our house began to undergo a metamorphosis. From one day to the next wonderful fragrances wafted through the air. One again the Advent wreath appeared in the center of the table in the living room, always made from fresh greens. Germany may not have been able to offer much in the way of things we had been used to before the war, but evergreens we had, lots of them. The lovely aroma of the wreath mingled with the scent of four red wax candles attached to the wreath, one candle for each of the four Advent Sundays. Silky red ribbons were wound around its circumference, and tiny ornaments in bright, vivid colors were interlaced throughout the greenery.

From that day on, every Sunday in the evening, apples would be baking in the small compartment of the tile stove. Oftentimes, the smell of gingerbread baking in the oven in the kitchen circled the air, and the perfume of hot apple cider joined the other heavenly aromas. It was a good time to have a well-functioning nose and not to be handicapped by a winter cold.

All these little wonders of the season added joy and anticipation of things to come. The wreath was not the only adornment. Shiny, red satin bows, red and gold candles and sweet-smelling evergreens were placed in every available receptacle and in every nook and cranny. My grandmother knew how to celebrate the season.

Then there was the Advent calendar especially purchased for me. These calendars with their 24 little windows carved into the scenery, one window for every day before Christmas, were meant to make the waiting easier. And every morning when I was allowed to open a window the countdown continued. I have to admit, nosy as I was, I often opened a window before its predestined date, and promptly had difficulty closing the window without the adults knowing it had been opened.

Little golden cherubs hung from the evergreen branches and made the branches almost look as festive as tiny Christmas trees.

Each Advent Sunday had its own little festivities. As soon as darkness fell one candle on the wreath was lit. Then our family would gather around the piano, my grandmother would begin to play all the old beloved carols, and we would sing. It was difficult to match my grandmother's beautiful soprano voice, but we tried.

During the days, and after school, I would run through the apartment more or less a nuisance. Sometimes, the other occupants of this large apartment house could hear me singing Christmas carols. Now I can only imagine what they were thinking. But no one ever complained.

The war was over, but not quite for me. Even during those wonderful Advent days, my father's absence was never far from my mind. We still did not know anything about my father's fate and no one could tell us. We did not know whether he had been taken prisoner or had been killed in action, a thought I vehemently brushed from my mind. I was convinced that my dad was coming home, no one could tell me otherwise.

My grandparents did their best to make the Christmas season as cheerful as they could. I was treated to a trip to the Opera House in Oldenburg to see Humperdinck's Haensel and Gretel. The Theater in Solingen did not have this opera in its repertoire in the first years after the war, so my mother and I made a special trip to the farmland up North. My family was adamant to make me forget about the horrific times we had experienced.

This event was pure enjoyment for me and many other young children. The auditorium was filled with children of all ages, anxiously awaiting the telling of the fairytale set to music by the composer. After the opera and the deafening applause had ended, we were given a special surprise. St. Nikolaus entered the stage, accompanied by his helper, Knecht Ruprecht. St. Nikolaus was dressed in a long red cloak and a miter on his head, he looked absolutely splendid. The Saint's helper was not always welcomed by all children. He carried a huge tome in one hand and a switch in the other. The story goes that the book contained all the misdeeds of children everywhere, and if a child had been especially unruly that year, the child's rear end would come in contact with the switch. It never hurt, the Knecht was always gentle with the admonition. I must have been an exceptionally well-behaved child that year, I did not receive a switching. But I often wondered how did he know who deserved the switch.

St. Nikolaus is the German version of Santa Claus, but actually not a part of Christmas itself. Germans celebrate this beloved Saint's day on December 6th. On the evening of December 5th children would place their boots or shoes outside their front door or, in our case, outside the living room door of the apartment, and in the morning the children would find the shoes filled with candies, marzipan or even chocolates. In this particular year, I was content with an apple and a few hard candies. At least the Saint had not forgotten me.

In Oldenburg, we were then given small gifts by Saint Nicholas, and he and the Knecht left the stage to return the following year on December 6.

It was a wonderful afternoon. My mother and I visited friends on the farm, and we were invited to a wonderful feast. Then we returned to Solingen.

Winter vacation did not start until one week before Christmas, and I was expected to finish my homework until then. I always thought it would be wonderful if school could be over for that year from December first to January second. That really would have made the Christmas season extraordinary.

After the tedious homework was finished, I spent a lot of time with my new friend. On those days when the cold winter air made it unpleasant to play outside, we busied ourselves with enjoyable things to do inside my grandmother's warm living room. I loved to design clothing for my paper dolls, my friend collected glossy pictures with lovely Victorian images. We would also fashion little handcrafted gifts for our families. At other times, our exuberance would prompt us to dance around our living room, hers or mine, all the while singing songs more or less in tune.

The war had taught us a valuable lesson. We were well aware how frail and fleeting life can be, we were happy to be alive and we were able to celebrate another Christmas without the danger of falling bombs.

Remembering those days, it is almost unfathomable how two families lived in such close quarters. Our new neighbors became our best friends, and somehow it all worked. And to my grandmother's credit, she never complained about our less than perfect living conditions.

162

The hallway of our apartment was shared by both families, and during this time the hallway held a peculiar attraction on December 24th. That day brought sheer enjoyment and excitement.

I would arise as soon as I was allowed, most likely at the crack of dawn. On that day, I prepared my own breakfast of oatmeal, I ate in the kitchen because on that day, the living room was off limits until the early evening hours.

My friend was already waiting for me in the hallway, she had the same rules. At one point during the day, we were both deposited in the kitchen with the door closed and no peeking allowed. My grandmother kept watch for a few minutes to make sure we stayed in the kitchen. That was the time when my grandfather brought the Christmas tree from the basement into the living room. The tree had been sitting in the basement waiting for this occasion. My friend's family did the same.

On that day, my friend and I had developed a particular attraction for our hallway with its doors and keyholes. But all our attempts at stealing a glimpse into the mysterious happenings in our living rooms were thwarted. The keyhole had been covered from the other side.

All sorts of cryptic noises came from those rooms. Dainty bell tones would ring, subdued laughter and whispering could be heard all through the day. Several of both our family members were hard at work in those living rooms, and try as we might we were not able to understand any of the conversation. The adults knew how to keep us children in suspense.

We could hear music coming from inside, and we could hear my grandmother's lovely voice accompanying the radio. During that day we did not see much of our families, other than the occasional emergence of one of them coming from that as yet forbidden territory. They were bombarded with question such as, "how much longer?" or "what were those bells?" The answer to that question was, "that was an angel visiting." Well, we were children and believed what they told us. But if that was really true, that angel

163

would have to have flown into the room through the window, because absolutely nothing would pass by us girls in the hallway unnoticed.

Every so often we would go into the kitchen to get a drink of water or eat a sandwich, but for the rest of the day we had Christmas Eve hallway duty.

Finally, at dusk, the long-awaited moment arrived, my friend and I parted company to start our individual Christmas Eve celebrations.

My mother would step into hallway, and I knew the long wait was finally over. She would brush my hair and make certain that not too much damage to my "Christmas dress" had been done, which I had been wearing from the moment I got out of bed that morning. The door to the living room was opened wide.

There in all its splendor stood the Christmas tree. What a glorious sight to behold. Flickering yellow wax candles lit up the room with a lovely warm glow. Sparkling ornaments were distributed all over the tree. It almost seemed as if the tree was aware of its beauty with its outstretched arms welcoming us to enjoy the moment.

Next to the tree stood a table covered with a large white cloth. I knew there were all kinds of surprises yet to be discovered under that cloth. This cloth became somewhat of a tradition even in later Christmases. I remember one Christmas where this cloth could not hide the outline of a long wished-for bicycle.

All five of us would assemble around the piano, and either my mother or grandmother would play "Silent Night, Holy Night", and we would sing – all three long verses. I love this carol, but at that moment three verses seemed like an eternity.

My friend, on the other side of the wall suffered the same fate, albeit with a different carol, but still with all three verses.

After the singing had been absolved, the cloth was lifted. A lot of happy shouting followed, with equally enthusiastic hugging and kissing and, "thank you, this is just what I wanted", though this was not always the total truth. Most of the time I really did like the gifts my family had chosen for me.

Then the adults opened their packages, including the small gifts I had fashioned for them. Seeing my family's faces when they opened these little inexpensive gifts, I thought giving really is better than receiving. Although I really did love my bicycle.

After everyone had settled down a bit, my grandmother served dinner. On Christmas Eve, it always consisted of pickled herring in cream sauce with apples and walnuts. I think we took this recipe from the Scandinavians.

The herring was spooned over boiled potatoes. With all the rationing going on then, it was a miracle my grandmother was able to put this meal on the table. We loved the herring and there were never any leftovers.

The star of the Christmas Dinner was always a goose, and that was served on Christmas Day. When I saw this perfectly brown and glistening bird on its platter, I remember thinking how glad I was that we had farmer friends.

Christmas Eve was a wonderful and joyous affair in our house. After dinner, I sat down next to the tree on a little footstool I had placed there. I gathered the books I invariably had received, and immersed myself into the world of fairy tales, my favorite stories.

Even though it was a happy evening, I still could not forget my dad somewhere in a strange land. I wondered where he would spend Christmas and I only hoped that he was warm and unharmed and that he would be home soon. My dad was never far from my thoughts or from my heart.

At some point my friend and I met in the hallway again and compared our gifts until it was time to go to church.

Later that evening we dressed in our warm winter clothes, hats, mufflers and boots and braved the cold winter night to attend Midnight Mass in our beautiful Gothic church just blocks away from our home. The church had been restored to a point where parishioners could attend services. The steeples were totally destroyed during the raid in early November.

The custom in Germany has been for many years that for holy days such as Christmas, Easter and Pentecost two days were celebrated. Stores were closed both days.

The second Christmas day in our family was reserved for visits from friends and relatives. This was also the day my grandmother was not allowed to cook or do any work at all. We all chipped in. My mother and her sister, Christl cooked, and I did the dishes. We were always amused at my grandmother's hesitancy to allow us to take over in her kitchen.

Visiting company was served whatever we were able to conjure up, usually pastry and cake and coffee. In the earlier post-war days, the cakes left much to be desired. And the drink was "Ersatz Kaffee", imitation coffee, made from grain. But whatever little we had, it was appreciated and we were all glad to be together again.

And so, another Christmas came to an end.

Conclusion

November 4th and 5th, 1944 about 2000 people died in Solingen and over 2200 suffered extensive injuries. The bombs on those two days were dropped by British fliers.

Fires still burned five days after the raids. Many people left Solingen to find shelter and housing in other towns.

In the days after the destruction, air raids still occurred regularly in Solingen. Most of those bombs did not hit the part of the town where my family and I found new living quarters.

Due to the raids, poor nutrition and worries about life after the war, people were in a constant state of distress.

The last raid on Solingen happened on April 13, 1945. From 1940 to 1945 over 27000 bombs fell on Solingen.

Made in the USA
Las Vegas, NV
23 January 2021